REDISCOVER
THE EVANGELINE TRAIL

A GUIDE TO NOVA SCOTIA
FROM YARMOUTH TO WINDSOR

PATTY MINTZ

Patty Mintz (signature)

NIMBUS
PUBLISHING

Nimbus Publishing Limited
PO Box 9301, Station A
Halifax, NS B3K 5N5
902 (455-4286)

Design: Kathy Kaulbach, Halifax
Photos: NS Economic Development & Tourism
Printed and bound in Canada

Nimbus Publishing acknowledges the support of the Canada Council and the Department of Canadian Heritage.

Canadian Cataloguing in Publication Data
Mintz, Patty.
Rediscover the Evangeline Trail
ISBN 1-55109-158-5
1. Evangeline Trail (Nova Scotia)—
Guidebooks. I. Title.
FC2307.M56 1996   917.16'3   C96-950013-0
F1037.M56 1996

CONTENTS

INTRODUCTION

My spouse and I were nomads long before the *Bluenose* ferry brought us to Nova Scotia, where we finally found our home. We had tried before to settle down, but somehow, the places that crossed our path never felt quite right—something always seemed out of kilter.

One hundred acres of woodland—beautiful in a rough and tumble sort of way—changed all that. We pitched a tent, dug a well, and began carving a niche for ourselves, with logs and rocks gathered from the surrounding countryside. Our well-intentioned attempt at homesteading in the rugged hinterland of Digby County, without the benefits of electricity and modern plumbing, was mixed with frequent forays around that inviting part of the province. In the process, we discovered a wonderful sweep of natural beauty and historical heritage from Yarmouth, along the Fundy side and through the Annapolis Valley, known as the Evangeline Trail.

Many years later, when the baby we had arrived with was ready for university, we moved once more, closer to Halifax, and began building again. Today, our house on the North Mountain near Kentville is fully equipped—modern wiring and plumbing and two more offspring—and provides us with a grand view of the Annapolis Valley.

I was excited about the prospect of writing this book, but unaware, initially, of how rewarding the project would become. As it turned out, I had been offered a gift—the ideal incentive to become still better acquainted with my own little corner of the world. In return, I gladly pass along the information and insights that were gathered and shared along the way.

Accompanied by my family, we began in spring, and by fall we had completed our final excursion, a time frame based on pragmatics, not premeditation. We were rewarded with an odyssey that, spanning three seasons, revealed a region rich with contrasting cultures and landscapes. Trees that were just beginning to bud were dropping their leaves on the ground when the final mileage was tallied and the task of translating our discoveries into the pages of a book began.

First-hand observations, and feedback from people encountered along the way, were combined with morsels of information unearthed from various sources, not the least of which being our invaluable regional library system.

A tiny wharf trimmed with a smattering of small fishing boats near Cape Blomidon, a lighthouse perched defiantly on a raw coastal outcrop of Brier Island, old earthen ramparts with a commanding view of the Annapolis Basin, a sprawling slab of straw-coloured marshland near Grand Pré; these are just a few of the places where we found it easy to imagine the land in an earlier, pre-asphalt era, unspoiled and flush with wildlife.

Even today the unsullied beauty is a strong attraction for visitors, and for people such as us who chose this place as home. We feel privileged that Canadians look here for their origins. The Mi'kmaq honoured Blomidon as sacred ground, home of their man-god Glooscap. Port Royal is revered as the first European settlement in North America.

There is something intensely pleasurable, almost addictive, about bundling some basics in the car, filling the tank with fuel, and heading off, with or without a preconceived notion of where you will end up. Our usual paraphernalia included good, sensible shoes (the kind grandmother would have loved), a map, binoculars, a notepad and some pens, a camera perhaps, and a bag of in-season fruit. Don't bog yourself down with too much clutter, we discovered, or you'll quickly become weary of rooting around through it all, rather too frequently.

Bear in mind that many of the places described here operate on a seasonal basis. For that reason, hours and opening and closing dates are often not included. In many cases, it would be wise to call ahead.

This book was not designed to promote one place over another, nor does it presume to have mentioned every destination worthy of note. Only, it aims to inform, and to inspire further discovery.

Patty Mintz
Centreville
Kings County, NS
November, 1995

COUNTY YARMOUTH

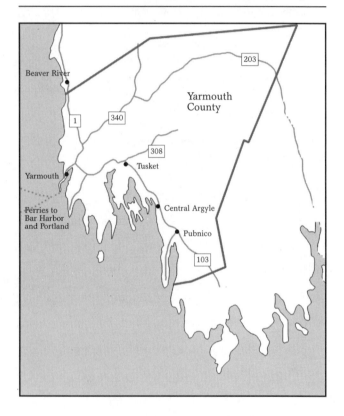

YARMOUTH

Since the turn of the century, when steamship lines began carrying passengers between here and Boston, Yarmouth has been one of Nova Scotia's busiest and most famous ports of entry, so catering to tourists has become both a business and a source of pride. This historical seaport puts on its best face for visitors to Canada as soon as they step off the ferry. The "salty" character of the old port area invites strolling, and although the shipping industry has diminished, shopping opportunities are abundant. Visitors can browse in stores that emphasize the contemporary and others that proudly boast a third-generation history.

The town has sprawled beyond its historic downtown into a suburban area dotted with malls, fast-food restaurants, car dealerships and other such modern day North American amenities. Fortunately, visitors see the old, distinctive seaport first. It's here that a once-booming shipping industry has left an indelible mark.

By 1879 Yarmouth had become the second largest shipping port, in terms of tonnage, in the country—this when Canada was the fourth leading maritime nation in the world. In turn, the shipping boom fostered other businesses and industries.

Fortunes were made from the spirited trade with New England and the West Indies. The region's newfound wealth brought a construction boom. Handsome buildings were raised along main thoroughfares and extravagant homes sprouted up, embellished with the fanciful ideas and materials seafarers brought back from around the world.

This time, cosmopolitan influence must have had great social impact on a community whose rusticity prompted the passing of a regulation in 1829 stating: "Ordered, that no pig or swine of any kind run at large on the streets or highways in the town of Yarmouth, within one mile of the church in either way."

The Information Centre by the ferry terminal provides a well-illustrated walking-tour guide generously sprinkled with facts and history. It describes a 4 km(2.5 mi.) excursion along Yarmouth's main and side streets, and mentions examples of Georgian, Italianate, Vernacular, Queen Anne Revival, Second Empire, Classic Revival and Eclectic architec-

6

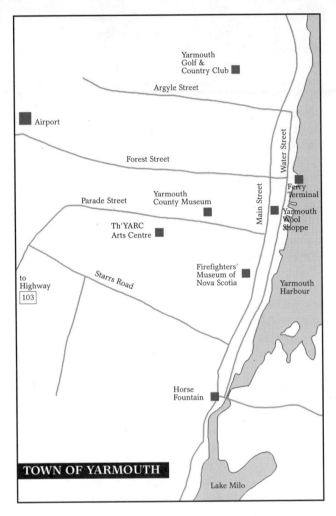

TOWN OF YARMOUTH

tural styles. Among other gems, you'll see the
family home of Mrs. Alfred Fuller (wife of the
original Fuller Brush Man), a rope-decorated,
Italianate house with portholes, built in the
1860s by a sea captain for his daughter, and
the Killam Brothers building, Canada's oldest
shipping office.

Main Street Yarmouth owes much of its
charm to Frost Park, the town's first burial
ground (some of the 200-year-old headstones

still remain), now an inviting place to rest your feet. A three-tiered fountain dedicated on the 100th anniversary of the town, wrought iron fences and a gazebo create a peaceful turn-of-the-century atmosphere. The local garden club lists Siberian pea shrub, goldflame spirea, threadleaf false cypress and American linden as some plants to watch for in the park and along your walk. The park was named for Sydney Frost, a Yarmouthian who became president of the Bank of Nova Scotia.

On the outskirts of town, cottage-rimmed Lake Milo attracts sailboaters, canoeists, swimmers and duck feeders. Near dark, we stood on the shore watching a gaggle of splashing children squeeze the last bit of daylight from a sultry summer day.

YARMOUTH WOOL SHOPPE

Where else would thick Fishermen Knit sweaters and heavy woolen socks sell briskly on a hot summer day? The Yarmouth Wool Shoppe caters to visitors from all over the world, but Scots may feel most at home surrounded by the racks of capes, shirts, jackets, skirts, tams, neckties and kilts in tartans and tweeds.

The store also sells authentic tartans in wool by the yard and books that help identify individual clan tartans (some clans have three tartans, one each for clan, hunting and dress). There are adorable, tiny tartan vests, kilts and skirts for toddlers, and a selection of British Burburry fashions including sweaters in camel hair and silky cashmere.

The classic woman's tartan kilts with knife-edge pleats and a shiny chrome clasp are as popular as ever, say the staff.

The shop—located in a Classic Revival style building on the corner of Main and Jenkins—is as distinctive as its merchandise, and owner Clyde Nickerson proudly bills the business as "Western Nova Scotia's most famous tourist store."

FIREFIGHTERS' MUSEUM
OF NOVA SCOTIA

How do you rescue three elephants from a fire? Yarmouth firefighters weren't fishing for a punch line when they pondered that question in 1963; they were pondering a highly unusual dilemma. Fire had broken out in the engine room of a circus boat docked in Yarmouth harbour just as it was preparing to sail. On board were leopards, bears, llamas, zebras, lions, a cheetah, trained dogs, horses, ponies and a Brahma bull.

See vintage equipment and artifacts at the Yarmouth Firefighters' Museum.

In the end, after a thrilling struggle and many acts of courage, all were saved with the exception of one zebra that drowned in the hold when the boat went down. The legend of the Circus Ship Fire was born.

Artifacts and photographs from the incident form part of an extensive collection at the Firefighters' Museum of Nova Scotia on Main Street. This is a wonderful place to visit with school-age children, not only because the museum features a shiny red 1935 Chev Bickle Pumper that kids are invited to hop upon and explore, but also for the many nifty doodads that pack the museum, including badges, lanterns, gleaming speaking trumpets, helmets and fire buckets and antique toy fire engines.

Besides that, the bright, shiny fire trucks have been so lovingly restored and maintained they look for all the world like full-size versions of the miniature metal cars and trucks some kids—and adults—have a passion for collecting.

We hadn't known that fire helmets serve not only to protect firefighters from head injury but also help to shed water from the back of the neck and are sometimes turned around to shield the face from intense heat; or that until the early 1800s the only way to fill fire engines with water was by the bucketful!

The museum's large collection speaks volumes about this revered profession. It's no wonder that many of those who visit are firefighters themselves, or have a family member or acquaintance in the profession.

The 1880 Silsby Steamer, the 1922 Ford Model-T Hose Truck, the 1920 Bickle Horse Drawn Pumper, and the 1866 Hunneman Reel with leather hose are just some of the antique apparatus that can set fire to vivid imaginations.

YARMOUTH COUNTY MUSEUM

"During the past few years a mania for collecting and preserving ancient records has prevailed to a surprising extent. This mania seized me as a child, and it still remains. Indeed, it appears to rage with greater violence as years roll on. I take no pains to find a specific to mitigate this malady. I rather enjoy it."

Physician James C. Farish (1811–1889) could have been speaking for today when he made that observation in his book about the Yarmouth of 1821. In our times, interest in the past is so keen that the Yarmouth County Museum on Collins Street has a full time archivist to help those researching history and genealogy.

The pride and joy of this marvellous museum is its more than one hundred paintings of ships, the second largest such collection in Canada. As well, there are photographs, model ships and such nautical artifacts as navigating instruments and various sailors' tools.

Downstairs, period room settings group the trappings of life in an olden days kitchen, bedroom, nursery and blacksmith shop. On the

Research your family tree at the Yarmouth County Museum.

main floor a Victorian parlour, in the typical fashion of that period, is wonderfully busy and elaborate.

A collection of exotic curios proves that Yarmouth seafarers were avid souvenir hunters. They brought back novelties that must have fascinated the people at home—Chinese ivory puzzles, Maori axe heads, an Australian boomerang and an ebony elephant from Ceylon.

YARMOUTH TO CAPE FORCHU

Directions:

From downtown Yarmouth, go north on Main Street. Turn left on Vancouver Street (at the gold and black Horse Fountain). Turn left at Route 304 to Overton, left again to Cape Forchu.

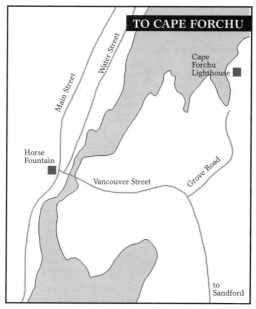

Images along the way of Cape Forchu and its famous lighthouse made us increasingly eager to get there. In Overton, we stopped to look at a monument marking the first launching in the county in 1764: "In proud memory of all the seafaring sons of Yarmouth County."

Fortuitously, the ferry from Portland, Maine, the *Scotia Prince,* pulled into view as we stood there. We all watched in amazement as the stately vessel made a left turn at East Cape and veered into Yarmouth Sound. Even the local clam diggers stop hacking the sand to watch the majestic ship manoeuvre its way into the inner harbour. Skilled navigation is required, because the inner harbour channel is at some places only 73 m (80 yds) wide, and the ferry is more than 18 m (20 yds) wide. The *Scotia Prince* glides by Battery Point and Lobster Rock Wharf before docking at the terminal in Yarmouth.

The Cape Forchu Lighthouse with the Scotia Prince *in the distance.*

At low tide the water doesn't just look shallow, it actually is, with often only .9 m (3 ft) of sea underneath the keel of the ferry—and occasionally even less.

Once, Yarmouth draped a banner over Main Street boasting of the fog. Well, why deny it? In summer, when sun-warmed air flows from the land and spreads over the cold water of the bay where moisture condenses and great, ominous fog banks are formed, Yarmouth can be fogbound for a week. It is a well-worn local joke that a "fog factory" is to blame. In one record-breaking stretch, the fog horn blew every day for months.

The sea eats away at Yarmouth Bar, where over the years the beach has gotten steeper and more exposed to the waves. This is a good place to pause and savour the ocean's energy, calmer on the Yarmouth Sound side, wilder towards the Gulf of Maine.

Cape Forchu, "Forked Cape," was aptly named by Samuel de Champlain when he spied the grey points of land as he sailed up the Bay of Fundy in 1604.

The treacherous fog and the less than ideal harbour begged for a lighthouse, which was finally built in 1840. It has since been replaced by a modernistic concrete tower, not popular with local residents who weren't keen for the design. An automated mercury vapour lamp of 2,000,000 candle power sends a beam of light thirty miles out to sea. The keeper's residence has become a station that monitors twenty automated lighthouses between Digby and Port Medway.

The jewel-like lens from the original light can be seen at the Yarmouth County Museum. It is the brainchild of French physicist Augustin Jean Fresnel (1788–1827). The lamp was surrounded with prismatic rings of glass mathematically cut to focus all of the rays into one beam that cast a bright light far out to sea. The lens had 360 prisms, weighed approximately £3,300 and cost a stunning sum for the times—$38,000. The lens was floated in a vat of mercury and rotated by weights that had to be wound every three hours each night. The lightkeeper had to climb several narrow stairways to the top of the light to perform this vital task. Sometimes, on very cold nights, the clockwork stopped, and the keeper of the light had to spend the night in the tower turning the light with a stick.

At the end of the road, there's a spectacular view of the harbour. The undulating surface around the Cape Forchu lighthouse is an irresistible invitation to scramble over the thick basaltic lava flow that covers fragmentary rocks.

According to geologists, these formations record the build-up, erosion and rebuilding of volcanic islands.

We were there in the morning, and the quality of light gave the place a surreal air. But this is a magical place to visit at any time of day.

YARMOUTH TO BEAVER RIVER

In Nova Scotia, the transition from city to country can be sudden. The scurry of town life faded quickly as we headed north along the coast on Highway 1.

The coastline from Yarmouth to St. Marys Bay has a raw, rugged feel. Sand beaches backed by dunes alternate with muddy bays surrounded by salt marshes. Plants such as the colourful Plymouth gentian, and others that are believed to have survived the ice age in offshore areas now covered by the sea, compose the Coastal Plain flora.

It's easy to see the violent influence of the wind, which shaped the coastal landscape, dwarfing and twisting trees into contorted sculptures.

All life here comes under the sway of the

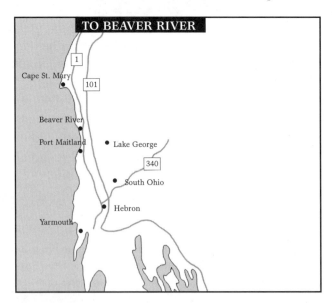

sea. Farmers do battle with poorly drained soils and an abundance of bogs; wet meadows spiked with blue-joint grass and white and black spruce, balsam fir and larch struggle against the salt air and hardpan land.

Further inland, where the extreme climatic influence is diminished, coniferous forests grow thick and hardy. The Tobeatic Wildlife Management Area, together with adjoining Crown lands, is one of the largest remaining wildlife regions in Nova Scotia. Bear and moose roam the rugged terrain in significant numbers. The area borders the 380 km^2 (147 sq. mi.) of Kejimkujik National Park, created in 1968 to protect and provide access to interior forests, bogs and lakes. A network of waterways allows exploration by canoe.

Closer to the coast, Lake George has breeding colonies of greater black-backed gulls and double-crested cormorants.

In his book, *Yarmouth County: A Naturalist's Notebook,* Charles Allen calls the Yarmouth coastline "An inextricable tangle of land and sea consisting of islands, capes, headlands, isthmuses and peninsulas as well as coves, inlets, sounds, bays, estuaries and tidal creeks. In many areas where mudflats and marsh margins are covered and exposed twice a day by the flowing and ebbing tides, it is impossible to say where land and sea begins."

SOUTH COVE NURSERY
Directions:
From Yarmouth, take Route 1 to Hebron, turn right on Route 340. At the Esso station in Ohio turn left at Richmond Road, then right at Brenton Road. The nursery is a fifteen minute drive or so from Yarmouth.

A gardener friend tells me that she's driven from her home (several hours away) just to visit this extraordinary nursery, which specializes in perennials and herbs. Over one hundred varieties of herbs flourish in a garden that's a joy for the senses.

The proprietors, Carla and Dave Allen, seem to know all there is to know about herbs. When herbs were needed for the movie *"A" The Scarlet Letter* (filmed in Shelburne in 1994), the Allens were asked to provide them. They also put out a marvellous little catalogue filled with information on preserving, cooking and growing herbs, and tips for making herbal wreaths, jellies and potpourri.

Some herbs, such as teasel, which attracts bees and butterflies, are primarily for show. Others, like feverfew, which relieves headaches, are known for their healing properties. Costmary sounds like an all-purpose wonder; it's used as a fragrant bookmark, insect repellant, in potpourri and as a tonic tea for colds, upset stomachs and cramps. The crushed leaf can also be used to soothe bee stings, or as a culinary herb.

Edible flowers such as calendula, whose bright yellow and orange petals can be added to omelettes or salads, or used in skin lotions, are another specialty. The couple says that a growing interest in natural treatments will probably lead them to expand their operation.

The home-based business has no set hours, but during the busy season, from April to July, someone is nearly always there. However, if you are making a special trip, it's probably best to call ahead.

Among other things, their garden-gift boutique sells books, bird and bat houses, bug shirts, loon whistles and herbal vinegars and jellies.

THE YARMOUTH CANDY COMPANY
Directions:
The Yarmouth Candy Company is located in Port Maitland at the corner of Highway 1 and Richmond Road.

Port Maitland has a lovely provincial beach park with a sand and pebble beach backed by a grassy picnic area—an ideal spot for nature-lovers—and a factory that makes sponge toffee, bon bons and peanut butter crunch—a perfect place for candy-lovers.

Visitors to the Yarmouth Candy Company can tour the factory to learn how barley toys, ribbon candy and chicken bones are made. Free samples add to the enjoyment. The gift shop sells bags of "quality handmade candy" including fudge, peanut brittle, butterscotch and chocolate specialty items.

Although some concessions have been made to progress over the years, the company boasts that "most of the recipes and methods are the same as they were more than a century ago.

THE DUCK POND INN AND
THE SPACE BARN MUSEUM
Directions:
From Yarmouth, turn right at the Beaver River Road. The inn and museum are a short drive in on the right.
What's a NASA space scientist doing in a place like Beaver River? "It was a 'stop the world I want to get off' kind of thing," explains Harry Taylor, a former atmospheric physicist for the Goddard Space Center in Houston, who decided several years ago he wanted to try something different.

He and his wife, Tina, found their escape in a tiny coastal community sitting on the Yarmouth-Digby county line. They began restoring a beautiful old house and started thinking it might be fun to have a bed and breakfast on the side. When word got out about Mr. Turner's credentials, he was encour-aged to share his experience and collection of space memorabilia with the public.

Why do we go to the planets? What is the

importance of space research? Why is it relevant to our concerns for the earth? Those are some of the questions the personable Mr. Turner addresses during a two-hour guided tour that is an essential component of the presentation. The Space Barn Museum, true to its quirky name, is housed in a beautifully renovated, attached barn and includes exhibits of space equipment and instruments, and a planetarium-like display. (Taylor remains active in his profession as a consultant to NASA).

The nature of the museum makes it unsuitable for casual drop-in visitors; groups of ten or more are required, but guests of the Duck Pond Inn, an upscale establishment that offers a gourmet breakfast with fresh baked croissants, queen-size four poster beds and a quiet pastoral setting with lake and ocean views, receive a complementary tour of the space museum.

COUNTY DIGBY

THE FRENCH SHORE

Exactly where the Municipality of Clare, or the French Shore, as it is more commonly known, starts and ends is open to conjecture, but the cultural mystique becomes strongly palpable as you approach Salmon River on Highway 1. The distinctive flag of the Acadians flutters from doorways and mailboxes—red for blood, white for purity, blue for the sea and one lone large gold star for the Blessed Virgin. Signs advertise salted onions, smoked fish, handmade quilts and that favourite Acadian dish—rappie pie.

Fishing settlements hug the St. Marys Bay

coastline while inland roads roll by secluded communities, gradually shrinking into logging lanes and hunting trails. Temperatures moderated by the ocean reduce winter and summer extremes. Inland, the snow piles high, but coastal villagers rarely need to shovel.

Nova Scotia's largest Acadian community, called *la Ville française* (French Town) by older generations, treasures a bond that is geographically close and emotionally strong.

No wonder the area stretching from Salmon River to St. Bernard has been touted as North America's longest main street. It's hard to tell where the dozen French-speaking villages that are closely clustered along a 40 km (25 mi.) stretch begin or end. The hospitality, too, is continuous—in restaurants, antique stores, folk art, cafes, service stations, inns, food markets, craft ships and churches of astounding grandeur.

Bilingual inhabitants descended from the first European settlers who came from France after 1632. In 1755 the British deported the Acadian population of Nova Scotia. Many drifted to Louisiana where they became known as Cajuns and developed yet another distinct culture.

Oral tradition has it that Acadians (escaping the deportation order) first appeared in this region in 1755-1756, but that harsh conditions killed many of the small group led by Pierre "Piau" Belliveau, who spent the winter on an island off present day Belliveau Cove. The first permanent Acadian settlers used the island as a burial ground from 1771 to 1791 in memory of that winter. Care is still given to a chapel erected on the site in 1890.

Most of the Acadians who were granted land in the township of Clare had been living in the Annapolis Valley before 1755. By the mid-1770s, thirty or so families had settled along the St Marys Bay coastline on

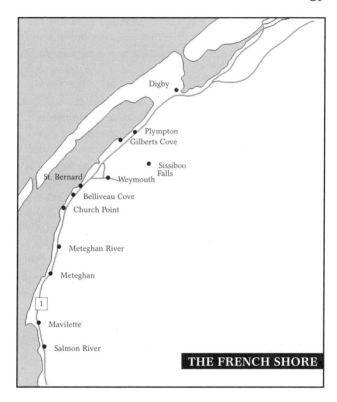

The French Shore map showing locations: Digby, Plympton, Gilberts Cove, Sissiboo Falls, St. Bernard, Weymouth, Belliveau Cove, Church Point, Meteghan River, Meteghan, Mavilette, Salmon River

THE FRENCH SHORE

government land grants; each allotment had water frontage, a marsh lot on which hay could be harvested and a large woodlot.

MAVILETTE BEACH
Directions:
Turn left off Highway 1 at John Douchette Road to get to Mavilette Beach Provincial Park.
The beach is known for its boardwalk-sheltered sand dunes, and as an excellent areas for shell hunters. About 250 different shell species are found in local waters, with about one hundred of these washing up regularly on the shore.

Past generations, especially youngsters, may have found dunes to be great places to play—ideal for climbing, sliding and digging.

Today, the dunes are recognized as fragile eco-systems, composed of sand bound by thin soil and a network of plant roots. Constant trampling by foot or motor vehicle causes the system to "blow out," or erode, to the point where winter storms can destroy them. Dunes are found in areas where beach sand is plentiful from eroding headlands and oval hills known as drumlins. Strong wave action piles the sand into a ridge, or berm, at the top of the beach. The addition of more wave-washed and windblown sand eventually builds into a dune.

There was a chill in the air when we arrived at Mavilette Beach, but a group of teenagers dressed only in shorts and T-shirts seemed unconcerned as they prepared for a party—some of them piling cases of soft drinks on picnic tables, while others were down on the beach pounding in posts for a volleyball net.

Drawing on their courage, we put on our bathing suits and headed for the water—a healthy hike at low tide. Our feet padded gingerly over the hard-packed, wind-rippled sand as the brisk wind became colder. When our toes finally touched water, our determination went up in a shiver. Chastened, we dressed warmly and spent the morning scouring the shore for shells and playing in the fine, packable wet sand.

METEGHAN

This is the busiest port along the Acadian shore. Only an experienced eye can tell the difference between trawlers, herring seiners, scallop draggers and the boats used to fish for cod and lobster as they slip in and away from the wharf.

Watch for the brown provincial park sign before Meteghan, which leads to Smugglers Cove. During the prohibition era, rum-runners used the cove and its high gaping caves to unload and store illegal alcohol. Wooden stairs have been built for observation. One short flight leads to a fenced-in viewpoint of the cliffs, caves and stone beach far below. The other is a challenge to the legs and lungs that takes you down to the shoreline.

La Vieille Maison is a monument to the lifestyle of nineteenth century Acadians of the region. The original house, belonging to the family of Louis Robicheau, an immigrant to Port Royal in 1636, was destroyed, but the present building from the same era was acquired and moved to the ancestral site, to be opened as a museum. The museum was designed to have a lived in feel and to reflect a typical well-appointed Acadian homestead—scrupulously clean yet comfortable. Family heirlooms and antiques from the region include sea chests, rawhide chairs and cooking utensils. During July and August, Acadian guides in traditional costumes offer information on the museum and surrounding area.

It was a rainy Sunday when we arrived in the area, so the famous shipyard of A. F. Theriault and Son a few miles north of Meteghan River was strangely quiet. A newly built car ferry, the *Joe Casey*, looked forlorn in the holding pond, waiting to be hauled across the bay to Brier Island.

Run by four brothers, this is the oldest and largest privately owned family run shipyard in Nova Scotia. The company began turning out three-masted wooden sailing ships in 1938 and now builds state-of-the-art fishing boats and finely crafted pleasure yachts, but the old skills of wooden shipbuilding are still used when building new boats and doing repairs. The company also has the facilities to build fiberglass and steel. Guided tours are available by appointment.

Massive breakwaters built with boulders the size of Volkswagens are common along the

French Shore. At the Saulnierville Wharf the breakwater towered over the fishermen struggling to secure their boats in the driving rain. We watched their labours from our warm car, while drinking mugs of steaming tea and feeling twinges of guilt.

The wharf was designed with perforated sides to help cushion storm waves. Built in 15 m (55 ft) concrete sections and floated into place, it was, nevertheless, an inadequate attempt to thwart the power of the sea. A massive round rock breakwater was needed for added protection.

ST MARY'S CHURCH

If one were to perch at the top of the famed steeple of St Mary's Church in Church Point, rising 55 m (185 ft) from the ground, a large chunk of the province would be laid out in a grand, sweeping spectacle. Forty tons of stone serve as ballast for the tower, the tallest wooden spire in North America, which shoots up towards clouds, often disappearing in a shroud of fog.

A stroke of luck, or a miracle some say, saved the church from disaster shortly after it was built. A lighting fire destroyed 9 m (30 ft) of the original 65 m (215 ft) high steeple before rain extinguished it.

A stunning monument to the faith of the Catholic Acadians, the church where Mass is still celebrated, recalls the days when forests, not fish, were the mainstay of these coastal communities. The lumber industry dominated the economy before fishing began to boom. Wood from nearby forests was a cheap and seemingly inexhaustible resource. In 1903, an inspiring volunteer effort began when parishioners started building under the guidance of Father Pierre-Marie Dagnaud and Leo P. Melanson, a renowned local carpenter who could not read or write, but could follow the plans of a French architect.

Inside the 60 m x 40 m (200 ft x 130 ft) church, built in the shape of a cross, whole tree trunks slathered in plaster convincingly masquerade as marble pillars. Spruce walls and ceilings were covered in painted sailcloth.

Continually rocked by the forceful winds of St. Marys Bay, the gigantic church needs a watchful eye. One recent repair project re-nailed boards under shingles on south side walls because rusting nails were losing their grip during high winds.

When a scale model was built—without the help of the original plans—to commemorate the church's seventy-fifty anniversary, binocu-lars were used to count the rows of shingles in order to determine the exact height at which to place the miniature windows.

Situated on the campus of St. Anne's, Nova Scotia's only French university, the church was erected in just two years at a cost of $54,000. It also hosts a museum full of local religious artifacts, including old vestments, antique crucifixes, incense burners and baptismal fonts, photographs and documents.

At the church, guides dressed in eighteenth century garb greet curious travellers, many of whom arrive on packed tour buses from around the country.

BELLIVEAU COVE
ART & MINERAUX

Claude Chaloux combs the shore near Windsor for gypsum of white, grey, brown, blue and black, and takes the soft, carveable mineral to his shop in Belliveau Cove and chisels it into graceful human and animal forms. His clay sculptures are sometimes car-ried to the beach, then primitively fired using seaweed, dried straw and driftwood. The salt content of the combustibles along with sud-den gusts of wind can sometimes make pieces crack or burst, but Chaloux is philosophical:

"That is something I accept, because nature is being selective. I am always very excited when I pull my bowls from the fire."

Chaloux will, on occasion, give demonstrations on the beach. Combined with the immensity of the sea and sky, the artist likens the experience to "a kind of pagan ritual, in the pre-Christian sense of the word."

Art & Mineraux (on the harbour side, next to the barber shop) also sells minerals for collectors, crystals, fossils, jewellery and art, and crafts from twelve developing countries.

THE ROADSIDE GRILL

It isn't easy to find an empty seat in the Roadside Grill in Belliveau Cove early on Sunday, but we were lucky enough to beat the post-church rush. Modest in appearance, this is where the locals head for plates heaped with fried clams and fries, and rappie pie—the adored Acadian potato dish.

There's no middle of the road when it comes to "Rapure"—people seem to either lover it or loathe it. Grated potatoes squeezed hard to extract the juice are baked with butter, onion and bits of beef, chicken or clams. The resulting dish looks strange to neophytes. Some never get past the greyish colour and gelatinous consistency. Others love the full flavour, the crunchy brown crust and huge chunks of white chicken meat. It can be slathered with applesauce or molasses, or eaten plain.

The Roadside Grill also offers it with bits of surf clams, those unattractive yet flavourful mollusks, said to have provided life-saving nourishment for early settlers. Neighbouring Grosses Coques is named for the large edible clams that live in the sand below the low tide mark.

ST. BERNARD CHURCH

The young guide dressed in Acadian costume tells us that awed expressions are common to visitors of St. Bernard Church. The humble demeanour of surrounding communities does little to prepare outsiders for the spectacle that greets them here. Tough times and frugality may have governed daily existence, but when the Acadians built churches they worked with the mind-set of millionaires.

Douglas fir was hauled in from British Columbia to construct pews and walls, gorgeous pewter Stations of the Cross were shipped in from Montreal and the main alter was topped with a great slab of Italian marble weighing 570 kg (1,250 lbs). A pair of ornate oak confessionals and hand-painted statues add to the stunning impact, as does the sweeping choir loft fitted with a two thousand pipe Cassavant organ, still played each week at Mass.

When there was no way of getting around economic realities, however, the local carpenters, fishermen and farmers who built the gothic-style church relied on ingenuity bordering genius. Stove pipes were smeared with a plaster veneer to imitate stone columns and

The French Shore community of St. Bernard.

intricate chandeliers aren't really silver as they seem—they're painted wood.

At 65 m x 30 m (215 ft x 100 ft), the church seats 1,010, almost the entire population of St. Bernard. It took twenty years to haul the more than eight thousand blocks of granite from Shelburne using railcars and teams of oxen. A blacksmith stood ready to sharpen the hand chisels that were used to cut the blocks. Ninety-six tons of mortar was hand-mixed and manually hoisted to the ceiling and walls as coating for interior lathes, then scoured to simulate stone.

The project was a massive community effort that lasted from 1910 until 1942. Each summer a picnic was held to raise enough money to continue for another year.

WEYMOUTH TO DIGBY

From St. Bernard, Highway 1 moves inland, crossing the Sissiboo River at Weymouth, founded by United Empire Loyalists and home to descendants of a black Loyalist community.

Lumber trucks piled precariously with spruce, fir and hemlock still rumble through this village on their way to the sawmill on the hill, but the face and flavour of Weymouth as a real lumbering town has faded. Now in the hands of a large conglomerate, the mill used to be family owned and operated. In the old days, board feet were tallied by hand, and strapping men used monstrous hooks called "peevees" to jerk logs from the holding pond. At noontime millworkers scented with spruce sap mingled in town dressed in workboots and hard hats.

St. Thomas Anglican Church was saved from the wreckers ball by the Weymouth Historical Society almost twenty years ago. Now the building has a new life as the setting for well-attended afternoon teas Thursdays from July to mid-September. Sandwiches, sweets, coffee, tea and other refreshments are served by various community groups for the enjoyment of tourists and locals alike.

Canoeing Odysseys Ltd., based in Weymouth, offers wilderness canoe tours and sea kayak "experiences" designed for modern-day adventurers. Packages include a two-day "escapade," and a three-day "Old Growth Forest" tour.

After Weymouth, the strong Acadian influence continues to diminish as Highway 1 rolls past another succession of small St. Marys Bay communities.

GILBERTS COVE LIGHTHOUSE
Directions:
Eight kilometres (5 mi.) east of Weymouth, turn left off Highway 1 onto Lighthouse Road.
Pharology, "the science of lighthouse construction and illumination," was far from our minds as we cautiously climbed the near vertical stairway to the cramped little peak of the Gilberts Cove Lighthouse. Yet it's natural to wonder—where did it all begin? And who were the people who kept the lights?

One of the earliest lighthouses was built by slaves and guided ships into the Egyptian port of Alexandria. Huge piles of wood were burned atop the "Pharo," a square tower over four hundred feet tall that is reputed to have been in operation for more than 1,600 years. Canada's first lighthouse, a gigantic stone tower, was constructed at Louisbourg in 1733 and used coal fires and oil-fed wicks to light the shore. The prospect of their passing because of new technologies heightens the romantic appeal of traditional lighthouses.

At Gilberts Cove, "Willie Jane" Melanson kept the light for nearly half a century before he drowned in the cove, leaving the task to his widow, and afterwards, their daughter Louise.

During the Second World War, lightkeepers kept a vigil for U-boats and submarines off the coast of Nova Scotia with the help of coded messages broadcast on the radio.

After Louise died, the lighthouse was shuttered and left to decline until 1982 when concerned citizens obtained custody of the crumbling property, by then considered a community scandal. Windows and doors had been smashed, stair railings and steps had been used for bonfires, and a huge unofficial dump had accumulated on the grounds. The Gilberts Cove and District Historical Society spent two years restoring the lighthouse, culminating in the return of its original light, which had been sitting in a warehouse in Saint John, New Brunswick.

Now, a music festival is held each summer to raise money for building maintenance and to help celebrate the rebirth of the lighthouse as a heritage site and museum.

On the day of our visit, a cloudless, corn-flower blue sky and an unruffled sea offered a clear view of Digby Neck across the bay. At other times, fog or "brume"—a moody spectacle of fog and mist that results when warm moist air brushes the cooler coastal waters—covers the vista with an eerie shroud.

We were most curious to visit the Japanese Cultural and Language Centre, in nearby Plympton, but uncertain what to expect, because its very existence seemed so eccentric. But its founder, Tom Haynes-Paton, immediately put us at ease, and we saw at once how naturally his remarkable enclave melds with its environment. The desire for a peaceful lifestyle lured Tom, a native of the American Midwest who worked for many years as a missionary for human rights in Japan, to the quiet shores of Nova Scotia.

Here, on property that slopes gracefully from the highway to cliffs overlooking the bay, he has created a place where the architecture, customs, arts and food of Japan can be explored in a setting of "real yet gentle immersion." Participants experience a Japanese daily life environment that includes sleeping on tatami mats, eating with chopsticks at a *kotatsu* (barbecue pit) and waking to the exercises of Radio Taiso with the rest of Japan. The learning process was designed for those visiting Japan on business or vacation or going there to live. The centre also offers weekend workshops on special interests such as Japanese calligraphy and art.

In a little shop, Tom sells items from his own collection of Japanese woodblock prints and antiques, including kimonos, porcelain, furniture and lacquer ware. Following Japanese custom, we removed our shoes and enjoyed steaming green tea and rice crackers while exploring the gallery.

Among the hundreds of pieces, all unique to Japanese society and culture, we marvelled at a rare *oyome-no-tansu* (bridal chest) from the early 1700s, likely built from trees planted by the bride's family on her birth; made from paulownia wood, it has a false wall behind a locked drawer and a secret money box. Special handles enabled it to be carried by pole to the newlywed's new home. Original woodblock prints date from the 1600s to modern print-artists and range from $25 to thousands of dollars.

Tom is well-versed on the Japanese way of life and willing to explain everything from cooking with seaweed to the art of woodblock prints.

Apart from the Centre, Plympton is typical of other small communities flavoured by farming, fishing and logging and anchored with a post office, a convenience store and a church that stretch along the shore of the bay towards Digby.

DIGBY

Directions:

Take Exit 26 off Highway 101.

Each August Digby pays homage to an economic mainstay with Scallop Days, a week-long festival of music, parades, sailboat races, street performers, a woodsman competition (forestry ranks second in economic importance) and the crowning of the Scallop Queen.

How fast *can* a scallop be pried from its shell or a fish sliced into fillets? On the wharf, fishermen suit up in rubber boots, aprons and gloves to test their shucking skills. With those who make their living in the trade performing for the crowd, fluted, fan-shaped scallop shells pile up at lightening speed.

The festival ends with fishing draggers—decorated with lights—sailing along the basin under a cascade of fireworks.

Digby is a major ocean entry point to the province, attracting more than 100,000 non-resident visitors each year. The recently refurbished waterfront district makes the most of its seafaring history. People are eager to partake of the food, the souvenirs and the maritime scenery. The *Princess of Acadia* ferry arrives here from Saint John, New Brunswick, and when it docks, campers, cars and bus tours test the town's traffic flow and the speed of its waitresses.

We're glad that Ed's, a small, unassuming seafood takeout famous for its fried clams and scallops, has so far survived the recent invasion of several fast food establishments. An institution among area inhabitants who ought to know well turned out seafood when they taste it, Ed's has been family run since it opened sometime in the 1960s.

A huge, hand-operated bell has been mounted in front of the post office on Water Street as a testament to the town's seafaring heritage. Originally used at North Point, Brier

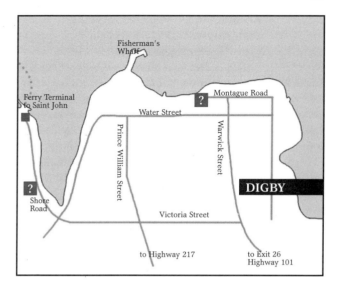

Island, in 1897 by the Department of Marine and Fisheries to warn mariners of the region's notoriously dangerous shoals, it has been etched with a small but powerful prayer: "Oh Lord thy sea is so great and my ship so small"—and a touching epitaph: "In proud memory of all the seafaring sons of Annapolis Basin, Digby Neck and Islands who were lost at sea during the period 1867–1967."

In the 1800s shipbuilders had their pick of prime lumber in surrounding forests and some put the plentiful materials, and their skills, to other good uses. One example is Trinity Anglican Church on Queen Street, built in 1878 and cited as the only church in Canada built by shipwrights. Designed by noted New England architect Stephen Earle, it has characteristics and materials—such as laminated arches, bracing and iron fasteners—common to wooden ships built a century or more ago. The churchyard, and the Old Loyalist Cemetery two blocks south, cradle the remains of Loyalist pioneers.

34

FISHERMAN'S WHARF AND
THE DIGBY SCALLOP FLEET

One of our first destinations in town was the wharf, hoping to see the celebrated scallop fleet, one of the world's largest with well over one hundred draggers. But the wharf looked lonely that day. Most of the boats, we were told, were out fishing on St. Marys Bay. Those that stayed behind were hunkered down on the low tide, roped snug to the wooden pilings. Some bore the names of women—wives, sisters or lovers?—on their colourful hulls.

Scallops are an institution and a year-round industry that have helped the region weather the decline in other fisheries—such as haddock, pollock, herring and cod—and the influence is everywhere. Local restaurants serve the succulent shellfish deepfried with french fries and coleslaw, simmered in hearty chowders and nestled in fresh baked rolls with tartar sauce (The Pines Hotel serves grilled Digby scallops with angel-hair pasta). But raw with a splash of lemon, some say, is best. Fishermen toss most of the mollusc away. It is the sweet, meaty adductor muscle (which opens and closes the shell) that people find delicious.

The Digby Scallop Fleet is one of the world's largest.

The Royal Fundy Seafood Market is wedged amongst three fish processing plants

at the entrance to the wharf—brimming with marine theme souvenirs, a live lobster tank and display cases piled with chunky halibut steaks, mounds of glistening scallops, sturgeon, haddock, smoked salmon and cod, salted pollock and tubs of Soloman Gundy (sweet pickled herring), which, on the shopkeeper's advice, we tried swimming in dill sauce. It was delicious—despite the styrofoam cup and plastic fork.

We left with a fistful of smoked herring, or Digby Chicks, as they're fondly called by the locals—so named, the story goes, because impoverished settlers used them as a replacement for chicken. Intensely smoky and salty, they proved instantly addictive. Dessert was pastel dollops of salt water taffy, eaten as we strolled through town.

THE ADMIRAL DIGBY MUSEUM

True or false? Some scallops have as many as fifty eyes, complete with cornea, lens, choroid coat and optic nerve. True, says the *Digby Scallop Cookbook,* a fund-raising project of the Admiral Digby Historical Society: "Around the edge of the fringed mantle, usually visible between the partly opened shells of the scallop, is a row of as many as fifty bright, shining eyes. They appear as dots of iridescent green encircled by rings of turquoise blue."

Available at the Admiral Digby Museum on Montague Row, the cookbook is a collection of history (for example, fishermen knew of the existence of scallops by the late 1800s but harvesting of beds in the Bay of Fundy didn't start until the early 1920s); trivia (scallops swim backwards by jetting water through an opening in the mantle); cooking tips and recipes. Local cooks contributed such diverse scallop-based concoctions as Scallop Chanterelles on Vegetable Fettuccini, Crispy Coconut Scallops, Scallops with Sauerkraut and Scallop Stuffed Peaches.

Situated on the western side of the Annapolis Basin, Digby was founded by New England Loyalist refugees who began sailing into the Basin in 1783 on the warships of Admiral Robert Digby.

Visit the museum to learn more about the history of the town and its nautical heritage through photographs, maps, costumes, theme rooms, genealogical records and special displays. In the Children's Room, a school scribbler belonging to Eugenia B. Cosman who went to the Digby Academy in 1885 reveals a student with neat writing and a talent for algebra. "Very good indeed!" wrote the teacher at the top of one page.

THE PINES

There wasn't a pine tree on the place when the original hotel was christened in 1903, but Henry Churchill thought the name would attract tourists. Churchill later ran into financial difficulties and the hotel was closed for a time, but in 1919 the Dominion Atlantic Railway secured an appropriation on the Pines for its purchase, repairs and improvements.

Under its new management, the hotel soon had more tourist business than it could handle. In 1928, building of a new Pines—a Norman-style chateau overlooking the Annapolis Basin —began. The following year the hotel opened under D.A.R. management with one hundred luxuriously furnished guest rooms. The same year work began on an eighteen-hole golf course. Today, the Pines is one of three resorts operated by the Nova Scotia government.

This is an elegant place to wash off the road dust and pamper yourself for awhile. In addition to eighty-three rooms and suites in the main hotel, thirty secluded cottages are spread around the luxuriant grounds. Guests can play tennis, lawn croquet or shuffleboard,

swim in the heated, outdoor pool, or play the par seventy-one, eighteen-hole championship golf course complete with a panoramic view of the sea. The course, designed by Canadian architect Stanley Thompson, winds its way past pine trees and over a meandering brook, which widens into golf ball-eating ponds on holes two and sixteen.

The elegant Pines resort offers many amenities.

The newly renovated Annapolis Dining Room serves everything from hot dogs to *Omble de l'Artic du Cap Breton Roche' aux Pistils de Safron* (Poached Cape Breton Arctic Char infused with Saffron Pistils).

DIGBY TO BRIER ISLAND
Directions:
To reach Brier Island from Digby, follow Route 217, boarding ferries at East Ferry on Digby Neck and Freeport on Long Island.
We felt a strong pull towards Brier Island, Nova Scotia's westernmost point and a haven for whale and seabird watchers. Route 217 meanders through the narrow peninsula of Digby Neck, always near the ocean. The waters of St. Marys Bay on the left and the Bay of Fundy on the right are never out of sight for long.

We were grateful for a clear, bright day, but

some say that only a good pea soup fog can create the right mood. Julia L. Sauer wrote her 1943 children's classic *Fog Magic* with Digby Neck in mind. Her young heroine, Greta, had a compelling affection for the fog that often wreathed her homeland.

The raw charm and unique marine culture of this almost completely undisturbed area are jealously guarded by those who live in its midst.

When developers proposed a super quarry at Eastern Head close to the Little River harbour facilities and a new deepwater port at nearby Porcupine Cove for the giant ocean-going ore carriers, concerned citizens formed The Society for the Preservation of the Eastern Head, a group that encourages non-destructive development of the region.

Thanks to their efforts, Route 217 was recently named "Digby Neck and Islands Scenic Drive." The society also works to protect rare, threatened and endangered Atlantic coastal flora that grow in the Digby Neck and Islands area. Significant stands of the threatened golden crest *(Lophiola aurea)* have been mapped on Digby Neck by scientists and naturalists.

Digby Neck, Long Island and Brier Island are the southwest end of North Mountain, a long ridge of basalt formed during the Triassic period that protects the Annapolis-Cornwallis Valley from the cool climate and fog of the Fundy shore. The mountain runs from Cape Blomidon in Kings County to the extreme western tip of Brier Island where it continues underwater as ledges and exposed rocks.

We didn't rush for the ferry to Long Island, which runs every hour on the half hour, because there are coves along the way to explore. Although similar to one another in many respects, each has a charm and character of their own, and some have intriguing stories.

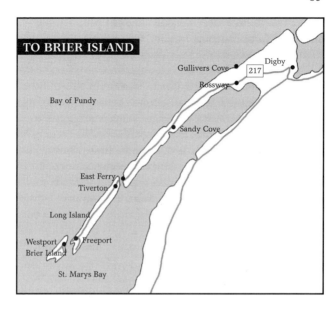

TO BRIER ISLAND

Bay of Fundy

Gullivers Cove • Digby
217
Rossway •

• Sandy Cove

East Ferry
Tiverton

Long Island

Westport Freeport
Brier Island

St. Marys Bay

At Rossway, we turned right off the highway and headed towards Gullivers Cove, a small, symmetrical undeveloped harbour named after the early pirate who is said to have buried treasure somewhere along the shore. "Cut-throat Gulliver," as he was fearfully called when he was out of earshot, met his end at the hands of his West Indian lover—a towering dark-skinned beauty decked out in pearls as big as chestnuts and a necklace of diamonds—when she buried her knife between his ribs.

Sandy Cove, nearby, is described rapturously by Sir William Dawson: "Whatever the causes of its present appearance, Sandy Cove is more like something a poet or painter might dream of than like an actual reality in our tame province of Nova Scotia."

"A safe and commodious harbour where vessels can ride the tempest safely," is how Isaiah W. Wilson described the same cove in his book on the geography and history of Digby County in 1893.

40

We agreed that it's one of the prettiest of the many coves along the coastline. Located midway on the Neck, its circular harbour by thickly wooded, emerald-hued headlands frames a view of the southwest shore of Nova Scotia across St. Marys Bay. The most intriguing local story we heard began at Sandy Cove when Jerome, as he became known, was found huddled on the shore there in 1866 with both legs surgically amputated and wrapped in bloodied bandages. Villagers on the French Shore took the mysterious castaway in and cared for him until his death in 1908 but they never found out who he was or how he came to be there, for he never spoke a word.

The sea is notoriously headstrong at Petite Passage, the half-mile wide gap between Digby Neck and Long Island, and Grand Passage between Brier and Long Islands. Almost four centuries ago explorer Samuel de Champlain tried to warn others of the hazards.

"The tides run strongly there, and chiefly at the little passage of the island, which is very dangerous for vessels that choose to risk its passage," he warned in 1605.

We put our complete trust—and a dollar toll—in the hands of our amiable ferrymaster, our bravery bolstered by usually calm seas and sunny skies. We got out of the car to savour the view and watch the aquamarine waters swirling in our wake, but the brisk wind and cold sea spray had us quickly reaching for our sweaters.

Despite the reputation of these waters, passengers should be reassured by the long history of the Tiverton Ferry, owned and operated by the Blackford family from 1822 to 1946 without a mishap. Until 1910, passengers were rowed across while their livestock swam alongside.

Tiverton, where the ferry docks, is one of

about thirty-five fishing communities and ports along the Neck, the islands and the mainland shore of St. Marys Bay. Historically, the ports have determined the settlement patterns for Digby County's 2,472 km^2 (955 sq. mi.) of land.

Ferry traffic creeps along thoroughfares lined with lobster traps. The Islanders are gifted recyclers. Cast off anchors, chains, nets and buoys adorn yards and doorways reincarnated as fences, birdfeeders, children's playthings and decorative art. Lumber thriftily salvaged from centuries of shipwrecks can be found in some of the older homes. The Islands Museum features items representing the heritage and family histories of the area.

Urged along by a pamphlet that warns, "The ferries are timed so that if you continue driving from the first ferry you will automatically connect with the second one: YOU DO NOT HAVE TIME TO STOP," we drove directly to Freeport where we were neatly packed on another ferry for the crossing of Grand Passage, an exhilarating twelve-minute trip ($1 round trip for cars, passengers are free).

BRIER ISLAND

What is it like to live on a small plot of land surrounded by the sea?

"Living here is no different from living anywhere else on the earth except to get on and off you have to work with the ferry schedule," explains Caroline Norwood, a writer who lives and fishes on Brier Island. "If it's stormy you may not be able to do either until weather moderates.

"The appeal would be the sea around us and all it has to offer—sounds, sight, smell, boats, fish, seaweed ... the beauty of it all, the solitude. You can walk the two-and-a-half miles on gravel road to Big Pond Cove and not meet a car or a person, only sea gulls or the

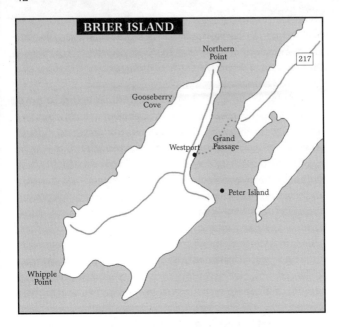

odd turkey vulture. Absolute solitude, which
is hard to find. Then someone on an ATV
comes screeching along flinging dust and
gravel and you swear. But mostly it's nice."

Revealing also are the statistics that show
the Brier Island public library has the record
for most books borrowed per capita from all
provincial libraries.

Westport, where the ferry docks, began as
a fishing station in 1769 with the arrival of
two families, the Welches and the Morrells.
About fourteen years later the population took
a sudden jump when eleven Loyalist families,
whose names remain today, settled along the
shore.

In the 1898 *Geography and History of the
County of Digby,* the island is described as "4
miles long, 1 1/2 wide ... the westernmost
land belonging to Nova Scotia. Thickly settled,
finely adorned and picturesque, Westport is
one of the foremost fishing stations on the
western coast—."

Today fishing has declined, tourism has grown and lobstering has become the big income earner for most people living on the island.

From the island's southern point, the dab of land known as Peter Island looks like a giant's stepping stone leading to Long Island. Have your binoculars in hand. Peter Island, named for a former keeper of the lighthouse, is a protected nesting area for Arctic and common terns during June, July and August.

Nearby, a small stone memorial perched on a grassy knoll honours the memory of Captain Joshua Slocum, the first person to sail around the world alone. Slocum, who was lost at sea in 1909, spent eight years of his childhood in Westport.

From the memorial, a well-worn hiking trail leads to the cliffs of Green Head. Nineteenth century geologist Abraham Gesner, who was shipwrecked on Brier Island as a young man, was intrigued by the basalt formations, and wrote: "The columns form long ranges of pillars, like the steps of the stairs, reaching from the sea below to the precipice above, which the waves often dash with fury."

Look for rare plants, precious stones and sea treasures while exploring Brier Island.

The shoals surrounding Brier Island are littered with shipwrecks. Sixty went under before World War II. In 1846, an especially bad year, only nine out of more than twenty-five vessels loaded with lumber for southern ports made it past the shores.

The island's only paved road, Water Street, just a few miles long, runs the length of the village from Southern Point to North Light. The rest of the island is accessible by dirt roads and hiking trails.

We headed to Northern Point for a look at one of the island's three lighthouses, then west to Pea Jack Cove whose raw, primitive beauty reduced us to silence. Signs of tide-borne litter aroused our beachcombing instincts, so we crunched our way over the sun-dried kelp, stopping to stir small tidal pools with our fingers and turn over tide-polished rocks. Finally, we made our way back up the steep embankment to our car, clutching our treasures—two small sea-shined engine parts to plunk into our flower bed.

On Brier Island wild flowers grow abundantly and range from common tansies to rare tiny orchids. Most trees are coniferous, stunted by strong sea winds. This is home to some of Nova Scotia's rarest plants, including the Eastern Mountain Avens, which grows nowhere else in Canada. Plant diversity is high: eleven species of orchids grow within sight of each other. Everywhere we went in this protected ecological environment, we saw wild irises clinging bravely to crevices.

WHALE WATCHING

Whale watching is hot on Brier Island. Eco-tourists flock here to experience a once in a lifetime thrill: humpbacks, fin and minke whales are sometimes almost close enough to touch.

The superior fishing grounds of Brier and

Long islands have lured sailors for centuries. Whalers, however, chose not to establish a processing station along the islands so whaling didn't become a major local industry. Today, whales stimulate an industry of a different, kinder nature.

Take a marine cruise and experience the thrill of whale watching.

In June, humpback whales, drawn by the rich marine habitat, begin arriving from winter breeding grounds in the Caribbean Sea, and with them arrive hoards of people hoping for a look.

Marine cruises have given the local economy—long suffering from the severe decline of inshore groundfishing—a big boost. In 1984 Carl Haycock, an American whale researcher and photographer, came to Brier Island to study humpback whales. Two years later, he joined with Harold Graham, an island resident, to offer whale watching cruises to the public, an endeavour that helps finance BIOS (Brier Island Ocean Study), a non-profit organization committed to studying whales and seabirds in the area. Since then, a few other cruise companies have started up.

Reservations and warm, waterproof clothing are essential for these remarkable trips. If you spot no whales during your cruise (a rare occurrence), expect a raincheck. Sightings of finback and minke whales, harbour porpoises and whitesided dolphins are common; beluga, sperm whales and other cetacean species have also been recorded.

The rarest of the world's whales with a population of only about 350, the North Atlantic Right Whale has a critical habitat in the Bay of Fundy off Digby Neck. The region between Digby and Grand Manan is a summer-fall Right Whale nursery.

Brier Island has lodging, places to eat, gift shops and booty for rockhounds: quartz, amethyst and jasper.

DIGBY TO BEAR RIVER
Directions:
From Digby, head east on Highway 101 towards Halifax. Smiths Cove, the long-time resort community, is located at Exit 25. For Bear River, turn right at the Joggins Bridge, then take the Lansdowne Road

BEAR RIVER
Bear River has a "sixties" feel. Twenty years ago the area was a refuge for city-weary young people, some from the United States, who came here in search of an "alternative" country lifestyle. Some stayed, some left, but the community is still known for its thriving population of artisans and "unconventionals." We spent hours exploring the unique shops and other points of interest in this picturesque village.

"The most photographed store in Nova Scotia," looks like a throwback to the hippie era, and is the home of Oddacity Designs, a retail store featuring the work of recycling artist, Zoe Onysko. She makes one-of-a-kind clothing, jewellery and conversation pieces from cast-off materials. Onysko is a virtuoso at turning unwanted velvets, silks, linens, brocades and other fabrics into beautiful yet comfortable jackets, dresses and robes. She also creates glorious hand-painted silk clothing. Most pieces are priced under $50.

Was it "the challenge to find non-linear uses for the mountains of discarded consumer goods," as Onysko muses in her flyer, that lead her to launch this unusual business? Whatever the reason, Onysko believes that opera buffs to Bob Dylan fans to "women who are tired of trying to look like their mothers" will enjoy the store, as will anyone with an offbeat sense of style and humour. But she warns: "This is definitely *not* the place to buy souvenir T-shirts or lobster key-rings, or to get your ego stroked by paying too much for something."

The Riverview Ethnographic Museum, open all year except for October, is another place to see marvellous clothing and fabrics. Turn left at the post office in the centre of town, then proceed to the fork in the road. Bear left on Chute Road and watch for the

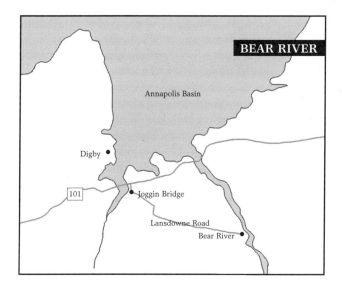

second house on the right, a large Victorian, #18. The proprietors boasts the largest collection of ethnic dress in any private museum in Canada. Also on the premises, The Costume Rental Shop offers everything for the discriminating masquerader, from Elvis to Elvira.

RETURN OF THE TOYMAKER

Warren Paton runs a hands-on, working toy shop where kids can make their own wooden toy for only $2 and where sawdust on the floor is a cheerful reminder that this isn't Toys "R" Us.

Designed as an "old world toymaker's workshop," Return of the Toymaker sells original design, handmade wooden toys, including German doll kitchens, village country stores, puppet theatres and a limited edition Noah's Ark. All of the pieces, notes Paton, are made from local hard and soft woods and are numbered and dated.

Almost as great an attraction as his toys, Paton loves to involve children and adults in his passion. Most kids jump at the chance to turn the crank on the antique hand-operated drill press, cut wooden dowels with a coping saw and pound pegs with a mallet. Paton drew oohs and aahs from a cluster of amazed onlookers when he used a rumbling one-hundred-year-old foot-powered scroll saw to cut an intricate Christmas ornament from a flat square of spruce.

FLIGHT OF FANCY

Flight of Fancy has been a mainstay in the village of Bear River for many years. The work of more than one hundred professional artisans is displayed in this wonderful shop.

It would be impossible to describe here everything in the store, but some highlights include the Birds of Canada painted on stone, sculptured hardwood burls, pottery, woven goods, jewellery and traditional Mi'kmaq crafts—and emphasize again that there is much, much more to be seen. The second floor art gallery exhibits the work of well-known Nova Scotia painters and sculptors.

BEAR RIVER SOLAR AQUATICS

Why are all these tourists wandering through a sewage treatment plant on a beautiful sunny day? Their curiosity has lured them from more likely holiday pursuits to Bear River Solar Aquatics, a wastewater treatment facility plunk in the heart of the village (next to the landmark Dutch windmill).

Visit the many unique shops of Bear River, featuring the work of local artisans.

It's easier to understand why people from Louisiana or British Columbia would want to devote some of their precious vacation time to sewage treatment as soon as you spy the well-kept greenhouse that houses the facility.

The interior is noticeably odour free and there is a pleasant tropical feel: banana and fig trees, irises and marsh grass, duckweed, pennywort, creeping primrose and algae, parrot feather and hyacinth are just some of the plant life that helps turn sewage into clean water by using natural ecosystems to remove contaminants and nutrients.

Close your eyes; listen to the relaxing murmur of water; feel the bright sun pouring through the polished glass panels. It's easy to imagine yourself at some tropical resort.

Here, sewage is more than waste material. It's food for the biological community that lives in large plastic holding tanks, an indoor solar pond and an engineered marsh. Snails and small fish are part of the process too.

The end result is to return treated water to the river—a welcome improvement on the days when raw sewage went pouring in.

The staff at the government-funded plant—the first of its kind in Canada—is so enthusiastic and the facility so inviting that it's easy to see why Solar Aquatics has become a tourist attraction. A more conservative community than Bear River might not have imagined that a sewage treatment plant had promotional potential. The village, including the board of trade, which donated the land, welcomed the unusual venture—and has obviously made the most of it.

Once a thriving shipbuilding centre, Bear River now moves at a much slower pace. For years the village was quite self-sufficient, producing its own newspaper and never lacking a doctor in 125 years. On the map, Bear River straddles the counties of Digby and Annapolis with the village bridge providing a visible boundary line.

Bear River (named for an early explorer, not the animal) is famous for its annual Cherry Carnival, and promotes itself as the "little Switzerland of Nova Scotia" and although the area may be short on snow-capped mountain peaks, its panoramic views and alpine atmosphere justify some license.

COUNTY
ANNAPOLIS

ANNAPOLIS ROYAL
Directions:
*Take Exit 22 off Highway 101, and continue east
on Highway 1.*

Annapolis Royal is a haven for history buffs.
In summer, the town is kinetic, energy
charged by visitors curious about Canada's
roots. Those who marvel at primitive cooking
tools and firearms, or who are touched by a
coarse piece of homespun cloth will find it an
exciting place to be. Where else can a casual
stroll take you down the oldest town street

and past the oldest wooden house in Canada?

Four of this country's oldest frame buildings still stand here, despite siege, demolition and three major fires. One hundred and fifty buildings in Annapolis Royal have heritage protection.

The Historical Association spices up walking tours with costumed actors performing historical vignettes. If you prefer a self-guided tour, pick up the brochure (at the "lighthouse" in the centre of town) "Footprints with Footnoes," which provides an excellent map of the downtown area. It lists almost thirty destinations, including the privately owned 1708 deGannes-Cosby House (said to be the oldest wooden house in Canada), the 1712 Adams-Ritchie House where Sir Thomas Ritchie, one of the Fathers of Confederation, was born, and the 1836 Court House with its whipping tree, a stately French Willow where lashings were once administered to petty criminals.

St. George Street, one of Canada's oldest thoroughfares, is the ideal setting for an eclectic collection of cafes, restaurants, museums, pubs and shops selling everything from upscale antiques and gifts to handmade chocolates, leather, pottery and books. The waterfront boardwalk offers peaceful respite and a pretty place to walk off supper.

We're glad to find that the exuberant King's Theatre, where we watched a young k.d. lang perform years ago as a newcomer, is thriving. The theatre offers a great variety of live entertainment, films and an annual summer festival.

Once in town, visitors gravitate towards Fort Anne, a commanding presence located only a few steps from the downtown shopping district.

FORT ANNE
It is ironic that a former military stronghold has become a place of wonder and learning, and that a summer day can be spent

pleasantly touring one of the most fought over pieces of land in Canadian history—the scene of lengthy conflict between England and France for control over Nova Scotia.

Standing high on Fort Anne's earthen fortifications, among the oldest historic features in the national parks system, the thought of young soldiers desperately defending, or attacking, the fort is chilling, yet the beautiful Annapolis Basin spread out before us is so serene.

Two young boys jarred the quiet mood with shouts and laughter. They had discovered that the squat, sombre powder magazine was perfect for a game of hide-and-seek, and that it was a wonderful echo chamber. Built in 1708, it is one of only two surviving original buildings on the site and the oldest building in any national historic site in Canada.

Two decades after the English destroyed the original Habitation down river at Port Royal, one of the earliest European settlements on the North American continent, the French returned, settling here, at the junction of the Allain and Annapolis rivers, where they began building a new Port Royal.

New attacks were launched by the English

The Officer's Quarters and impressive grounds at historic Fort Anne.

each time war broke out between England and France. In 1710 the fort fell a final time. The area was renamed Annapolis Royal, while the fort became the official capital of Nova Scotia after the Treaty of Utrecht ceded mainland Nova Scotia to the British.

In 1749 the capital was moved to Halifax and the fort was gradually downgraded to an outpost. The last detachment of troops was withdrawn in 1854. Forty years later towns-folk organized to preserve some of the crumbling structures.

Outfitted as a museum sixty years ago, the 1797 Officer's Quarters houses an exciting new centrepiece exhibit, the Heritage Tapestry. Even Queen Elizabeth II lent a hand in creating this 2.5 m x 5.5 m (8 ft x 18 ft) work of art—adding a ceremonial stitch. With vibrant colours and bold images, the needle-point tapestry was created to commemorate and interpret the four-hundred-year history of Annapolis Royal, in particular Fort Anne and Port Royal. Older children especially will find this an appealing history lesson.

Parks Canada staff and scores of volunteers spent five years working on the painstaking project, designed by Nova Scotia artist Kiyoko Grenier-Sago. The work consists of four panels, one for each century. Fort Anne and nearby Port Royal charge an admission fee, a worthwhile price to pay for experiences such as these.

HISTORIC GARDENS

The sweeping entranceway, where an admission fee is collected, couldn't contain the sensual floral fragrances that greeted us as we left our car. By the time we started our tour, under the protection of the towering Linden tree near the gateway, we were inhaling great draughts of nature's perfumes with utter abandon.

Our tensions seemed to tumble as we

wound our way slowly through the sumptuous grounds. Four hectares (10 acres) of gardens, 2.8 ha (7 acres) of reclaimed marshland and a 20 ha (50 acre) wildfowl sanctuary fanned out before us.

The handy little map that we'd been provided with guided us around the lush environment. This is a wonderful place to take a leisurely afternoon stroll. Nearly everywhere we turned people were bent forward, closely admiring bush and bud.

The Historic Gardens were established in

1981 as a living monument to gardening and horticulture in the area. The gardens overlook wetlands and meadows where European settlers began cultivating crops almost four hundred years ago.

The colourful and well-tended grounds at Historic Gardens.

We ached with envy of the carefully tended flower beds, thinking of our pale efforts at home. Neither have we eight full-time gardeners. But the gardens weren't always this way. "Before and after" photos in the Interpretive Room show its gradual development.

Chrysanthemum, delphinium, hypericum, iberis, gloriosa daisy, astilbe, feverfew, liatrus—the exotic names match the beauty of the plants. The granite rock garden contains other intriguing varieties, such as sedum, creeping thyme, dwarf iris, cat mint and spiderwort.

Fossil remains show that roses grew 35,000 years ago, but they would surely have paled beside today's hybrids. After four thousand years of cultivation, modern gardeners tend varieties of roses unimaginable to the Egyptians, Persians, Greeks, Romans and Chinese, all of whom were fanciers. (Ancient Greeks cultivated the Damask rose for its oil. The musk rose was prized during the rein of Queen Elizabeth I.)

At the Historic Gardens the sequential development of roses is a sensory adventure. More than two thousand bushes represent over two hundred cultivars, from the oldest species to the modern grandifloras.

Among other delights are the early Acadian cottage and potager (vegetable garden), the Innovative Garden, the Winter Garden, the Pine Forest, the Acadia dyke replica and a Spring Colour Garden.

The Gardens Gift Shop and The Secret Garden Restaurant operate on the grounds, which are open from May through October.

ANNAPOLIS TIDAL GENERATING STATION
Directions:
The tidal station is situated on the Highway 1 causeway northeast of Annapolis Royal, just past the fire hall.

The moon is for romantics, but lunar power is put to more practical use at the Annapolis Tidal Generating Station, the first and only modern tidal plant in North America.

We know that the gravitational forces of the moon and sun create the tides, but what fuels our passion for playing with the limitless power of the ocean? Civilization's search for clean, renewable sources of electricity, for one.

Opened in 1984, as an experiment, the station engages the largest straight-flow turbine in the world to generate enough electricity to power 4,500 homes. Built on a small island in the mouth of the Annapolis River, the station takes full advantage of the powerful Bay of Fundy tides, the highest in the world.

Wicket gates resembling venetian blinds arranged in a circle open to let water flow through the massive, four-blade propeller turbine, the largest of its kind by almost 4 m (13 ft). As the runner turns, the rotor's magnets sweep past the wire coils in the stator creating an electromagnetic current, which is tapped and converted at a nearby substation to become usable electricity.

The Annapolis Tidal Generating Station, the first and only modern tidal plant in North America.

The process is a fascinating lesson in the ingenuity of modern applied science. An interpretive centre, which also serves as a tourist bureau, offers details and a peek at some of the operating components.

A local environmental group invites visitors to enjoy the "Foam Show" around the Annapolis Causeway and the tidal power plant. Like a bucket of soapy water, the Annapolis River foams when it is shaken. The surprising phenomena is the natural result of extreme turbulence and dissolved organic matter. On a windy day foam billows across the causeway, staining the river and its tributaries brown with humic and tannic acid. The substances wash into the waterway from coniferous forests producing organic matter that is resistant to decomposition.

ANNAPOLIS ROYAL TO VICTORIA BEACH

Directions:

Continuing past the tidal generating station on Highway 1, turn left at the intersection at Granville Ferry.

Along the way to Victoria Beach, the highway rolls past lovely old homes, (a few of which have been turned into splendid lodgings) museums, artisan shops and plenty of places to simply stop and enjoy the Annapolis Basin view.

Over the North Mountain, the Delaps Cove Wilderness Trail offers a 9.5 km (6 mi.) (round trip) hike that winds along secluded forest clearings and a rocky shoreline. The trail has become a favourite place for family nature hikes.

The system consists of two trails. The 2.2 km (1.4 mi) Bohaker Loop opens onto the Bay of Fundy shoreline and leads to a 13 m (43 ft) waterfall while the more rugged 7.3 km (4.5 mi.) Charlie's Trail offers several look-offs along the coast. There are also stone foundations of a black community that once existed in the area. Both trails are well marked and offer interpretive signs along the way.

NORTH HILLS MUSEUM

Antique fans will find the North Hills Museum in Granville Ferry fascinating, with its dazzling collection of antiques bequeathed by Robert Patterson to the Nova Scotia Museum in 1974.

Patterson was a Toronto banker before he retired in the mid-50s and opened an antique shop in Yorkville, Ontario. Later, he bought and restored a circa 1764 "saltbox" wooden farmhouse in Granville Ferry as a showplace for his extensive collection of furniture, ceramics, glass, silver and paintings, mainly from the Georgian period (1714–1830).

The pieces, ranging from a walnut chest and a "Japanned" desk to Spode porcelain and portraits by John Hoppner, George Chinnery, Sir Francis Chantrey and Francis Cotes (all were members of the Royal Academy of Arts in London), are displayed as they were when Patterson resided within.

The house was named for the forested North Mountain, which forms a lovely backdrop for the old property.

THE PORT ROYAL HABITATION

By their second winter, residents of Port Royal, the earliest permanent European settlement north of Florida, were probably bored to distraction. They needed something to lift their spirits and help sustain them through the long, tedious months of cold and dark along the Annapolis Basin. So Samuel de Champlain formed for them one of the earliest social clubs, *L'Ordre de Bons Temps* (the Order of Good Cheer) in 1606.

The purpose, Champlain wrote in one of his diaries, was to "keep our table joyous and well provided." Banquets and entertainment became weekly routines, and feasting rituals were established to enliven the all-male gatherings. The same winter, Marc Lescarbot, a Parisian lawyer who resided at the Habitation, wrote and presented a play called *Le theatre de Neptune* for the further enjoyment of the group.

The Habitation is a replica of the small French compound founded by Pierre Dugua de Mons, which operated as a fur trading centre from 1605 to 1613. It was reconstructed by the Canadian government in the 1930s based on drawings by Champlain illustrating buildings grouped around a courtyard and central well.

Experience 17th century life at the reconstructed Port Royal Habitation.

The settlement was home for about forty-five colonists including carpenters, shipwrights and sailors. Residents clutched at any break in the tedium, even turning, we're told, to the constant quarreling of a Catholic priest and a Huguenot minister for amusement.

When the men weren't trading furs or tending gardens, they must have longed for families and friends left behind in civilized France.

It's easy to see how "the blahs" quickly consumed the inhabitants of the small, sparse compound, and why few renewed their year-long government contracts, in spite of the fact that the settlement was ahead of its time with such creature comforts as wooden floors.

It's the rough simplicity, however, that makes the restored Habitation so exciting to explore. It's fun to poke about the sail-loft, the storeroom and winecellar, the cannon platform, the trading room and gentlemen's quarters. We especially liked the common room with it's massive fireplace big enough to roast a cow and long and weighty dining table. In the kitchen, the unwieldy equipment— ponderous bread dough paddles and hulking iron cauldrons—took muscles to hoist. Strength, not culinary skill, must have been a cook's primary prerequisite.

The Habitation experience is heightened by the presence of well-versed, highly enthusiastic guides dressed in workingmen's clothes from the period, including sabots, the inexpensive wooden footwear of the day.

VICTORIA BEACH

The road ends at Victoria Beach where, on a clear day and with the right timing, the *Princess of Acadia* ferry can be admired in the distance as she gracefully slips through Digby Gut into the Annapolis Basin and steams towards the ferry terminal in Digby. The ferry provides year-round service between Digby and Saint John, New Brunswick, three times daily during peak months.

From Digby Gut to the end of Brier Island, faults divide the basaltic ridge of the North Mountain into sections. Three of the faults are now found along water gaps, the deepest being at Digby Gut, which has been eroded out by the Bear River and by tidal currents. The second forms Petit Passage between the end of Digby Neck and Long Island. Grand Passage, between Long Island and Brier Island, is the third.

Not far from our ferry-watching spot, a roadside memorial reminded us that some earlier travellers didn't have time to spare daydreaming on this pleasant route:

> Between February and November 1849, a pony express carried dispatches containing European news from Halifax to Digby Gut where they were shipped to the telegraph station at Saint John and relayed to the press of the American seaboard cities. The Halifax Express covered the 146 miles in as little as eight hours with fresh mounts supplied enroute and rider changes at Kentville. This successful system, furnished by the Associated Press, was superseded by the extension of the telegraph to Halifax.

From now on, our daily newspaper will be read with a newfound respect.

THE ANNAPOLIS VALLEY

Rivers and glaciers scoured soft sandstones for millions of years to create what is now the Annapolis Valley, a lovely, extremely inhabitable region cradled between the North Mountain and the Southern Upland, and stretching 135 km (84 mi.) from the head of St. Marys Bay to the Minas Basin shore.

Laced with winding rivers, fertile farmlands, villages, towns and rural communities, the valley is doubly blessed, shielded by the North Mountain from the cold and foggy Bay of Fundy a mere five miles away.

At the western end of the valley, from Annapolis to Lawrencetown, there is a comforting intimacy in the narrowness of the valley floor and the nearness of the steep forested slopes on either side. From here, the valley widens from about 4 km (2.5 mi.) near Annapolis to about 14 km (9 mi.) near Wolfville.

This is the land that inspired writer Ernest Buckler, a native of Dalhousie West, who captured the essence of rural Nova Scotia life in his Canadian classic *The Mountain and the Valley* and other books.

BRIDGETOWN

Those who like to ogle other people's houses will enjoy a visit to Bridgetown, east of Annapolis Royal on Highway 1, where the architectural styles reflect a colourful history. Mi'kmaq, Acadians, New England planters and Loyalists all contributed to the development of this diverse region.

A 1986 building inventory of the town's main thoroughfare, Granville Street, identified twenty-five residences built between 1780 and 1850, thirty-seven built between 1851 and 1900 and twenty-four built between 1901 and 1913. Architectural styles include Greek, Gothic, Queen Anne and Georgian Revival, New England Colonial and Second Empire.

Yes, Bridgetown was so named for a bridge (built in 1803 to span the Annapolis River) and it does, as has been often observed, exude plenty of small town charm. While calling itself "the prettiest little town in Nova Scotia" may seem like an overblown boast, the area is undeniably home to some of the prettiest houses to be found anywhere.

Bumbleberry pie is an ingenious Canadian creation that inspires discussion wherever it is served. While ingredients may vary according to availability and the temperament of the cook, at the James House Museum and Tea Room on Queen Street, blackberries, raspberries, apples and rhubarb are tossed in a pastry shell, then baked until the amethyst juices bubble from under the tender crust.

Built in 1835 by Richard James, a merchant and Justice of the Peace, the building went on to serve as a home, a flower shop, a doctor's office, an art gallery and most recently a museum and tea room. Saved from demolition in 1979 and declared a Municipal Heritage Site, it offers a wonderful setting in which to enjoy a light lunch and a variety of home-made desserts.

Normally, travelling on main highways provides little scenery and less insight, but Highway 101 offers motorists almost a bird's-eye view of an unusual geographic feature; between Kingston and Aylesford, the road crosses one of the few inland sand dunes in Nova Scotia, affording a panoramic look at the narrow ridge of sand covered with pine trees, which stretches away on either side of the highway. The dunes are an accumulation of fine sand blown from glacial deposits.

THE ANNAPOLIS VALLEY EXHIBITION

The Annapolis Valley Exhibition is one place where the scent of manure is intrinsic to full enjoyment; farm animals, after all, are the crux of country fairs. After six days of competition involving the likes of goat showmanship, beef conformation, ox pulling and giant squash growing, audiences are sure to come away with a greater appreciation for local agricultural heritage and an unlikely affection for the earthy aromas that waft through the fair grounds on scorching summer days.

This popular fair, held in Lawrencetown each August, has come a long way since the days when its original predecessor, the United School Exhibition, charged a dime to admire displays of flowers, livestock, map drawing, sewing and other examples of rural proficiencies submitted by students from the Lawrencetown School District. Singing concerts, ball games and races accompanied the judging of entries, and the singing of "God Save the King" was the finale to the day's activities.

These days, big-name entertainers widen the "Ex's" appeal, while the Bill Lynch midway, introduced to the fair in 1929, adds the irresistible flashiness of a carnival, teasing crowds with games of chance and stomach-churning rides.

MIDDLETON

Directions:

From Highway 101, take Exit 18A.

Normally, watches and water don't mix, but in Middleton liquid is an essential ingredient in what is billed as "North America's first town water clock." Visitors can watch the

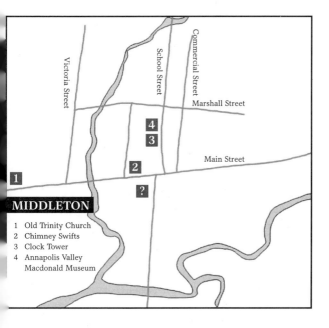

MIDDLETON

1 Old Trinity Church
2 Chimney Swifts
3 Clock Tower
4 Annapolis Valley
  Macdonald Museum

seconds drip away in a fascinating replica of an ancient flotation-syphon type of clepsydra. Coloured water, weatherproofed with anti-freeze, makes the workings of the device more visible and keeps it operational year-round.

Clepsydras were developed by the Babylonians about 1400 B.C., but fell out of use with the advent of the pendulum in 1656. Middleton decided that turning back the clock might help publicize the marvellous Macdonald Museum (which, incidentally, houses an extensive antique clock collection), and the town. So, the curious clepsydra was set up beside Town Hall.

An interpretive panel explains that water stored in a chamber on top of the clock slowly flows through glass tubing into a calibrated funnel to act as a time adjustment device. Once through the funnel, the water rests in a glass cylinder containing a float. As the chamber fills, the float rises, pushing up a rod containing cogs that mesh with the hand movements. When the cistern fills, a syphon drains the water into a storage chamber below, then an electric pump pushes it back up to the top.

In modern times, clepsydras are treasured for their beauty, not their precision. The Middleton water clock is an eye-catching creation of glass and brass that also has three other clocks built into it as a modern concession to accuracy.

THE ANNAPOLIS VALLEY MACDONALD MUSEUM

Believing that one-room country schools left much to be desired, millionaire tobacco magnate and educational philanthropist Sir William C. Macdonald chose Middleton as the testing grounds for an educational experiment in centralized schooling.

Photographs and memorabilia from Canada's first consolidated school, which was built with funds provided by Macdonald and which operated from 1903 to 1979, are on display in a re-created classroom at the Annapolis Valley Macdonald Museum, located in the original school building on School Street.

We expected to hear a din of tick "talk" from the clock and watch collection (there are well over one hundred), so we were surprised by the silence that greeted us. Most of the timepieces are in working order but left unwound, which somehow enhances their fanciful shapes and ornamentation.

Arranged according to case style, the collection is a testament to the imagination and craftsmanship of early clockmakers who were as much concerned with the beauty of the shell as with the inner workings. The oldest piece is a small Nathanial Hodges bracket clock, ebonized with gilt mounts and dating to the late 1600s.

The exhibit also includes a fascinating and comprehensive display that explains how mechanical clocks work and a delightful reproduction of a turn-of-the-century clock-maker's shop.

Many of the clocks were originally collect-ed by Norman Donald Phinney of Wilmot and eventually acquired by the Nova Scotia Museum. Clock design tends to reflect current trends in decorating, which makes them his-torically interesting as well as delightful to look at. The Macdonald Museum collection includes Ogee clocks (named for their mould-ing), looking-glass clocks, pillar and scroll clocks, steeple clocks, shelf clocks, mantel clocks, ship's clocks, novelty clocks and many others including, of course, the distinguished grandfather clock (so named for a popular old song that grumbled: "My grandfather's clock was too tall for the shelf...") Most of the time-pieces are regulated by pendulum, rather than spring driven.

Also of interest is the Rusty Nail Collection. Don't be deceived, as we were, by the name. Although the collection started in the late 1950s with just two old handcrafted nails, it now includes hundreds of historic artifacts, such as diverse household items, agricultural tools and books gathered by local school children.

The collection grew out of an unusual educational strategy by Middleton high school teacher Leonie Cumming, who tried to stimulated her student's interest in history by urging them to search for evidence of local pioneer life.

It quickly became clear that she had captured their interest; the classroom was soon groaning with objects scoured from attics, basements and barns, all now on display at the Macdonald Museum.

THE CHIMNEY SWIFTS

Bird watching is enjoying an explosion of interest, but those who prefer to observe from their favourite lawn chair, rather than traipse through field and forest, are especially fond of chimney swifts. Their penchant for roosting in vertical enclosures makes them an ideal subject of interest for modern day nature lovers, who need only sit back and wait for the birds to come to them.

In Middleton, residents successfully rallied to save an unused chimney at the regional high school (which was earmarked for renovations) because it is a favourite nesting spot for swifts. In the summer of 1995, one count recorded 450 swifts at the school on Gates Avenue. The show starts just before sunset and lasts for half an hour or so. (The town of Wolfville holds dear a swift show of its own.)

Chimney Swifts were well named. By day the speedy little birds fly out to feed, returning at dusk to their chimney of choice. Nearing home base, they may be flying at between 65 and 80 km (40 and 50 mi.) per hour, yet they can shift from forward flight to vertical descent in just a few seconds by changing the stroke of their wings. Fanning quickly back and forth overhead, the swift uses its wings like helicopter blades to lower straight down. Sharp claws grasp the rough brick surface and spiny quills on its tail feathers help prop the bird from below.

Crowds gather to watch the aerial display and usually linger a while to enjoy the evening air and the company of like-minded neighbours and visitors.

MIDDLETON TO PORT GEORGE
THE FAIRY TAILOR'S TEA GARDEN
Directions:

From Highway 101, take exit 18A if you're coming west from Kentville, Exit 19 if you're driving east from Digby. Follow the signposts to Port George, then follow the signs to the Fairy Tailor's Tea Garden, a short distance up a dirt road.
No matter how many times I cruise over the North Mountain towards the shore, it's always a delight when the Bay of Fundy jumps up to greet me at the crest, refreshing my spirit as I begin the slow, gradual descent to the water's edge. Travellers craving a serene oceanside experience can take their pick of dozens of tiny coastal communities hunkered along the Bay of Fundy. Most used to pulsate with shipbuilding, fishing and trade; today they lure citified folks to their shores with a promise of spectacular coastal scenery. Majestic landforms created from the combined effects of geology, glaciation and the powerful Fundy tides help compensate for the frigid water and lack of sandy beaches.

Visitors to Port George can enjoy the view from the patio of the Fairy Tailor's Tea Garden, a delightful place that specializes in gourmet foods seasoned with fresh herbs and edible flowers grown in the owners' luxuriant English country garden.

Its whimsical name suits perfectly its

location—a 150-year-old house hemmed by gardens and perched daringly on a hill overlooking the bay. The Tea Garden features dishes of homemade pasta, fresh seafood, free range chicken, lamb and assorted ethnic foods presented so as to be as much a feast for the eyes as the palate.

Mary and William Bell have grown accustomed to diners photographing plates resplendent with edible blossoms of calendula, nasturtium and violets before taking up their forks. Some say the breads alone, fresh baked from hand-milled grains, make the drive worthwhile.

Tables are set with fresh linen, polished silver and the couple's own collection of antique china. Mary sews and sells a lovely array of Victorian nighties, children's clothes and original teddy bears.

It's wise to double-check before heading over; the restaurant is seasonal and is closed several days a week to allow the husband and wife team plenty of time to cook.

COUNTY KINGS

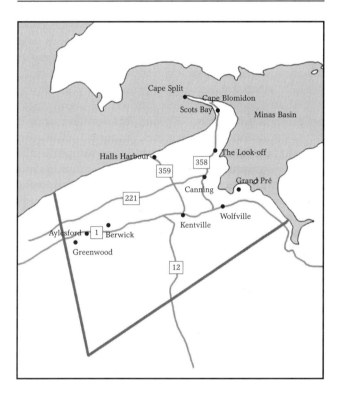

FARM COUNTRY

Best known for its apples, Kings County also accounts for 87 percent of the province's chickens, 90 percent of highbush blueberries, 85 percent of potatoes and 70 percent of vegetable crops. But we don't need statistics to tell us this is farm country. A cruise down practically any back road is proof enough.

Directions:

East of Middleton, on Highway 1 in Aylesford,

*turn left on Victoria Road towards the North
Mountain, then right on Route 221 heading east.
This road takes us through one of the province's
quintessential farming districts. As an option,
turn right in Aylesford on Victoria Road, then follow the blue zoo signs to the ever-popular exotic
animal zoo, Oaklawn Farm.*

OAKLAWN FARM ZOO

This family owned and operated zoo started as
a farm with a few exotic animals and birds
and has become one of the region's most
popular tourist attractions with over one hundred species, including the largest variety of
cats and primates east of Quebec.

The zoo's charm lies in its casual, farm-like
atmosphere, so appealing to school groups and
families. Owners Gail and Ron Rogerson have
successfully raised zebras, llamas, lemurs,
lions, jaguars and other animals. Animals that
are listed on the Species Survival Plan (SSP),
and the CITES list (Convention on
International Trade in Endangered Species)
reside on the farm. Between 75,000–100,000
people visit the zoo each year, but the
Rogersons say their prime purpose is not to
exhibit the animals, "but rather to give them a
home where they can be at ease."

Route 221 is beautiful any time of the year,
but in late May, when apple orchards are coat-
ed in a blizzard of fragrant white blossoms
blushed with pale pink, or in early fall when
the apple and pear trees are peppered with
fruit, when pumpkins are piled in farmyards
in enormous heaps, and leaves—maple, oak,
ash and elm—are just beginning to turn, the
scenery is sensational.

The road rambles along the foot of the
North Mountain, past century-old, family-
owned farm houses, pastures edged with
freshly painted fences, towering silos, old red
barns and sway-back sheds. Aylesford,

Dempsey Corner, Welton Corner, Welsford, Welton, Woodville and other farm communities, including Berwick, the "Apple Capital," coalesce for 30 km (20 mi.) or so. (Show patience for the slow-moving farm machinery that travels the road.)

Golden cornfields collide with apple orchards in various stages of growth: slender, shoulder-high saplings burdened with fruit too big for their branches and mature standard variety trees, gnarled and sturdy.

About twenty different varieties of apples are grown here; some land in pies, some end up as juice or sauce, but Cortlands and Macintosh are most prized for fresh eating.

Black and white holsteins share the pastoral neighbourhood with chubby black-face sheep, poultry and hulking draft horses whose only purpose now is to bring their owners glory at the local country fair.

In fall, when cornstalks turn brown and witch-like, U-picks swing into high gear, and little wooden farm stands, some no more than two planks on a saw horse or an old wooden cart, are bursting with all manner of produce—apples, pears, tomatoes and cukes, little sugar pie pumpkins, gourds, homemade butter—waiting to be loaded into the car for a fraction of the price paid in the city.

To delve deeper into farm country, turn left in Woodville at the flashing light onto Bligh Road, and proceed for about 2 km (1.2 mi.), then turn right at the Woodville Road and proceed for about 1 km (.6 mi.) to the Foote Family Farm.

Two friendly Jack Russell terriers hurried to greet us when we arrived at this picturesque 89 ha (220 acre) farm, where beekeeper and apple grower George Foote sells the fruits of his labour: honey, apple cider, Burbank and Early Golden plums, big, sweet eating-cherries and apples, apples, apples. The

U-pick season starts about mid-August with tart Crimson Beauty, sweet Astrachkan, Quinte and Paula Red and continues with Gravenstein, Macintosh, Cortland, Delicious, Russets, Cox Orange and others until the last apple is tugged from the branch sometime around Halloween.

A fourth-generation farmer, George can sometimes be found fussing around his bee-hives (he has four hundred but many are rented to blueberry growers for the purpose of pollination), extracting honey in huge stainless steel vats that rely on centrifugal force, or pressing fresh apple cider. If you'd like to know how bees spend their winter, or which apples store longest and make the best pies, just ask George.

Honey is sold in various quantities, from reusable little "salt and pepper" jars with holes poked on top, to 25 kg (55 lb) pails. We picked enough macs and cortlands to eat fresh all winter, and for spooning into preserving jars as thick, chunky fruit sauce and spicy apple butter.

Those who care to linger can stay over. Pastures around the farm double as rough camping sites.

HALLS HARBOUR
Directions:
From Route 221, turn left and proceed to Centreville. At the intersection, turn right on Route 359 for Kentville, or take a left to reach the historic Bay of Fundy fishing village of Halls Harbour.

In July and August, when the valley floor is hot and humid, people love heading to Halls Harbour where the cool Bay of Fundy breeze gives respite. From the shoreline, there's a good view of the Minas Channel, distinguished by the bottle-cap shaped Isle Haute to the left, the cliffs and lighthouse of Cape d'Or and Cape Chignecto straight ahead in the distance, and the unmistakable jagged silhouette of Cape Split far away to the right.

An unlittered gravel and stone beach, flanked by steep basalt cliffs capped with groves of hardwood and softwood trees, invites a closer look. Up above, erosion has eaten the ground right from under some tottering spruce trees, now precariously unsupported with half their roots bare to the elements. Kids love poking around the rugged beach terrain. Time has carved curious little cubbyholes, convenient footholds and dark, tiny caves along the basalt abutment.

Halls Harbour is one of many fishing villages along the Bay of Fundy settled by New England Planters and Loyalists. Smugglers and privateers were drawn here by the coves, ideal anchoring places along the rocky shore, and legend tells of buried gold and marauding pirates, one of whom the village was named for. Samuel Hall was a native of the county who returned from New England to raid new settlements in Kings County sometime around 1779. In one inland raid, it is said, he was cut off from his boat, chased overland to Annapolis and back to New England.

While the wharf needs repair, the surroundings are otherwise ideal for an eating experience aptly called "lobster in the rough." Based on the premise that the seaside scenery enhances flavour, the lobster pound offers them plucked fresh from local waters, boiled in a huge pot of boiling saltwater, then served conveniently precut with a plastic bib, eating utensils, melted butter and rolls. Painted picnic tables are scattered around the weather-worn cook house.

Fishing boats, lobster traps, swarming seagulls, the ever rising and falling Fundy tides and even the pungent marine aroma all seem to stimulate conversation as well as the appetite.

For the more adventuresome, who want to work up their appetites, two local sportsmen offer kayak tours from Halls Harbour, including one that lets romantics "paddle away to a secluded beach for a fresh lobster supper and return into a beautiful east coast sunset."

Today, lobster has become a pricey delight, but in the past villagers would go out after a storm and gather buckets of the plentiful crustaceans from under the pier to feed to their pigs.

A gift shop at the lobster pound sells souvenirs, and across the way an authentic country store, long owned by the Parker family, sells penny candy, ice cream and edible seaweed called dulse.

A small core of permanent residents contends with winter's icy winds, spirit-bashing storms and steep slippery roads; come spring the population swells as people return to air out their cottages and settle in for a lovely laid-back summer.

MARTIN AND NEVILLE STUDIO AND GALLERY

At the studio of John Neville and his wife, Joyce Martin, the art of intaglio printmaking is explained for the delight and education of visitors to the house where John, a former fisherman, was born. The couple specializes in limited edition prints that illustrate the history and lifestyles unique to the Bay of Fundy.

Many of the narrative pieces created from etched and hand-wiped copper plates are based on John's own upbringing in the community. Works such as his recent *Salmon Supper*—which depicts a traditional get-together in the local hall, where people piled their plates with rolls, pickles, vegetables and poached salmon caught in local weirs—portray the down-to-earth humour essential for survival along this rugged coast.

THE FAIRY-TALE COTTAGES
Directions:
From the Neville Studio, continue up the hill. At the top. turn right on Simpson Road and proceed for about 2 km (1.2 mi.), then bear right when the road forks.

We half expected to see the Seven Dwarfs and Snow White come skipping out of the whimsical stone and cement structures known locally as the fairy-tale cottages. Perched at the shore of Huntington Point, they were the inspiration of Charles Macdonald, a valley native born in 1874 who travelled the world then returned home to found the Kentville Concrete Factory. Macdonald liked cement for its durable, non-flammable properties. A confirmed socialist, he believed in helping his fellow man, so he put a crew of local men to work after the Depression building the five fancifully shaped cottages.

Over the years some structural changes have been made by various owners who still use the landmark cottages as summer retreats, but their distinctive charm remains intact.

KENTVILLE

Kentville is one of those lucky towns that enjoys the best of both worlds. Known as the business and professional centre of the Annapolis Valley—banks and investment firms abound, and the fifty-five-million-dollar Valley Regional Hospital complex was opened in 1992 to serve Windsor to Digby—it is also an oasis place of parks, hiking trails and nature sanctuaries as well as a great sports centre. In seasonable weather the local parks and ball fields are in continual use; soccer, baseball, slowpitch and hockey competitions draw hordes of exuberant fans to two of the best sports facilities in eastern Canada—Memorial Park and Centennial Arena.

On warm summer evenings, whole families

go to the park to watch the action from bleachers, lawn chairs or the hood of their car. The town's basketball and tennis courts and the public swimming pool are used to capacity by young athletes.

Kentville (named to honour the Duke of Kent who toured the area in 1794) has had a long love affair with sports—said to have started with the game of cricket in 1870. Soon

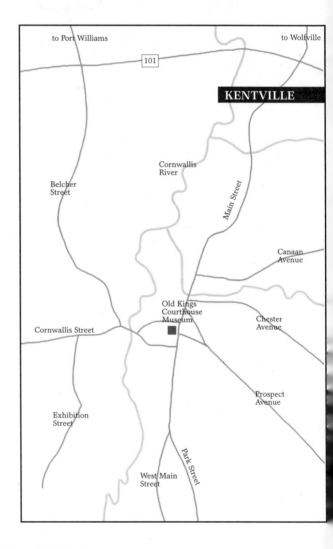

after, the town's first baseball team was formed. Football, basketball, hockey, tennis, curling and other organized sports followed. In local pubs, talk still turns to 1985 when Kentville won the National Baseball Championship.

THE TOURIST BUREAU AND OTHER DOWNTOWN DELIGHTS

When the trains stopped running through town (Kentville was once headquarters for the Dominion Atlantic Railway), the pretty little red-brick train station seemed wasted and forlorn, until the local tourist bureau moved in. Now it's busy once again, overseen by an enthusiastic staff.

Abandoned rail lines that cut through the centre of town will be converted (starting in 1996) to hiking trails linking the Kentville ravine at the eastern end of town, through the town centre, to the bird sanctuary at the western end along the Cornwallis River. Originally protected as a haven for migrating ducks, the sanctuary is a popular spot for local bird-watchers who can expect to find up to eighty different species, many familiar favourites such as chickadees, warblers, red winged blackbirds, owls and, in early spring and summer, perhaps a bald eagle or two.

One-way traffic circles easily through town, but the best thing to do is park the car and strike out on foot. Downtown Kentville has a handful of pubs, including one Irish-style establishment that brews its own beer. Taming the wilderness would have been less labourious if the early settlers could have slaked their thirsts and indulged their appetites at the likes of Kentville's pubs.

Edgemere Gallery in the Town Square Mall sells fine Atlantic-Canadian art and handcrafts and is always hosting a wonderful exhibit or two by renowned Nova Scotia artists such as Janet Pope, Holly Carr, Alan Bateman and Leonard Paul.

The Cornwallis Inn on Main Street shocked Depression-era citizens with an extravagant one million dollar price tag when it was completed by the Canadian Pacific Railway in 1930. Recently renovated, the towering, Tudor-style landmark now houses an elegant ballroom, restaurant and lounge as well as businesses and apartments.

OLD KINGS COURTHOUSE MUSEUM

Some people visit the Old Kings Courthouse Museum on Cornwallis Street simply to marvel at the astonishing patience of one local artist during a 1981 refurbishing project. Brad Forsythe stripped several layers of paint from the walls of the old courtroom, covered them with a base coat of white paint, then applied stain using traditional woodgraining methods from the past, which created the illusion of natural grain oak. The artist then added his distinctive signature by sketching a rabbit, bear, goat, fish and other animals into the wood pattern.

The red brick building, which served as the seat of justice and municipal government from 1903 to 1980, now houses records of King's County's social history as well as natural history displays.

Besides permanent collections that include a Victorian parlour, mounted birds and rocks and minerals from the Annapolis Valley, the museum has a well-used library and community histories archives. All of the county's 100 cemeteries have been recorded and indexed, and over 170 rolls of microfilm containing births, marriages, deaths, census records and other statistics useful for family history hunters are housed in the lower level of the museum.

When an invitation was extended in 1758

to the people of New England to help settle the fertile farmlands that had lain idle since the Acadian deportation, thousands jumped at the chance. Eight years later, about 8,000 "Planters" (an Elizabethan term for colonists) had already made the move. An exhibit commemorating these pioneers features kid-oriented, hands-on displays aimed at sparking young imaginations.

THE KENTVILLE RAVINE

The parking area off east Main Street that serves the 57 ha (140 acre) Kentville Ravine fills up quickly on a fine day. This is where local residents come when they want to really stretch their legs and lose themselves (not literally) on a winding, wooded trail. The hike isn't long, only about 4 km (2.5 mi.) round trip, but the dusky habitat (an old-growth coniferous forest composed largely of eastern hemlock, with scattered red spruce, beech, maple balsam fir, striped maple and white pine) and the meandering Elderkin Brook, over which the wide, comfortable footpath occasionally bridges, lead to a climactic end at a rushing waterfall that seems more than just a few miles from the bustle of nearby Kentville. Some of the grand, towering Eastern Hemlocks that distinguish the ravine have been dated to about 1755. A fire that swept through the area around the time of the Acadian expulsion burned earlier trees.

Red Squirrels scutter about the forest floor collecting mushrooms (some of which are poisonous to humans), to be stored underground or hung in trees to dry. They have plenty to pick from. This is an unusually rich fungal area.

Curious cave-like hollows of soft reddish sandstone have worn into the steep walls of the ravine. Biologists call the ravine "species rich" and consider it representative of forest environments that were once common in the region.

The ravine is part of a 101 ha (250 acre) parcel of land granted to the Nova Scotia Fruit Growers' Association by the provincial government in 1912 to establish an experimental station specializing in fruit.

Spectacular scenery, accessibility and the relative ease of the hike have made this a popular place, but be aware that the area is home to many fragile species of plant life including ferns, orchids and jack-in-the-pulpit that should be left untouched.

If you prefer solitude, walk the trail on an inclement day or during working hours. Nice weather brings out scads of walkers, many accompanied by children and the family dog. And by all means bring a snack. A sign along the trail points the way to a pretty picnic area above the ravine on the grounds of the Kentville Agriculture Centre. While you're there, it's worth visiting the Blair House Museum, which celebrates the history of the apple growing industry with photographs, artifacts and a peek inside a turn-of-the-century evaporating plant that made apple concentrate.

THE APPLE BLOSSOM FESTIVAL

Imagine the excitement when French settlers at Port Royal harvested Canada's first apples sometime around 1610. The trees would have been pampered and tended with care. Who could have forseen the long-term results? Almost a century later, over 1,500 trees were growing in the Annapolis Valley, and the Nova Scotia apple industry was well on its way to its present ten–eleven million dollar farm-gate value.

A smidgen of the three million bushels of apples produced each year in the province are transformed into imaginative desserts for the annual Apple Blossom Festival dessert contest. Local restaurants vie for the title of official festival dessert by creating confections such as apple blossom soufflé and apple almond phyllo crisps.

The competition is one of the early events leading up to the really big show (it's one of Canada's largest spring festivals) traditionally held at the end of May, when apple blossoms are at the peak of perfection. The coronation of Queen Annapolisa on Friday night is accompanied by a flurry of teas, art and craft shows, beerfests, concerts, fireworks and other gala events that carry on for five days.

Arrive early for the Grand Street Parade during the Apple Blossom Festival.

Routine life in Kentville and the immediate surrounding area comes to a screeching halt for the famous Grand Street Parade. At 12:55 P.M.—five minutes before the parade begins— exits 12 and 13 off Highway 101 are closed, and traffic on local roads is suspended. Hours earlier spectators begin picking their observation points, then guard them jealously. By the time the first floats lurch from the starting point at the town line, an estimated 100,000 people have positioned themselves along sidewalks, lawns, storefronts and rooftops. For two hours throngs of bagpipes, marching bands, majorettes, clowns and floats make a royal ruckus to everyone's delight. In the morning, before the main event, kids get a chance to grandstand in a parade of their own.

The festival was born in 1932 (partly to help publicize the apple industry in Europe and North America), when most of the eight million bushels of apples grown in the province came from the Annapolis Valley. While production has declined, the celebration remains as popular as ever.

When blossoms have turned to fruit, autumn is celebrated with equal enthusiasm. The last weekend of September is Harvest Fest time in Kentville, and in October, legions of amusing "pumpkin people" surface in wild and wacky poses.

From Kentville, head east on Highway 1 for the hub of the New Minas commercial district, a shopper's paradise, and the beautiful Ken-Wo Golf Course or west to Coldbrook where golf enthusiasts can play Par-three, miniature golf or practise on a driving range.

WOLFVILLE

Directions:
Take Exit 10 off Highway 101 in Grand Pré coming west from Halifax. Coming east from Digby, take Exit 11 in Greenwich.

Around 1830 Elisha DeWolf thought it a good idea to give the boot to Mud Creek, the name by which Wolfville was originally known. It's still kicked around in the name of fun, especially during Mud Creek Days when some events call for wallowing in the stuff, but a town of Wolfville's stature truly deserves a more dignified moniker.

Wolfville is largely defined by the omnipresence of Acadia University, founded in 1838. While some residents may grumble mildly as a flood of students doubles the town's population each September, the advantages of being a "university town" far outweigh the inconveniences. Acadia boosts the economy and attracts business and cultural events of a sort not usually found in such a small community—not to mention the dynamic, youthful energy the students bring.

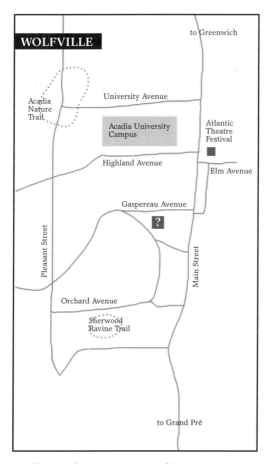

The 100-ha (250-acre) Acadia campus enhances an already charming town. Such diverse cultural events as Russian ballet, opera, and the Rankin Family (Celtic Nova Scotia singers) take place on campus, bringing together students and other townsfolk.

86

Wolfville is a town of walkers, joggers, bicyclers and carriage pushers. Residential streets shaded by towering elms invite relaxed strolls past sumptuous Victorian inns and some of the province's more elegant homes, including that of the town's most famous resident, artist Alex Colville.

The downtown business area is also full of architectural character and has an air of sophistication, thanks to the specialty shops that offer everything from imported clothing to gourmet foods. The Coffee Merchant and Front Street Cafe, two downtown coffee shops with patios, are popular people-watching spots. Even the local donut shop has class.

Wolfville's stores cater to the cosmopolitan tastes of its well-travelled, multi-cultural customer base, which is a great bonus for the locals too. Eos carries everything from chick-

The well-kept grounds and stately buildings of Acadia University.

peas to curry paste while the neighbouring Kitchen Door serves gourmet take-out dishes, including unusual salads, lasagna and quiche. Wolfville also has two well-stocked book-stores—Box of Delights and The Odd Book— and a discriminating video store, Light &

Shadow, where film buffs have a big choice
of foreign flicks and National Film Board
titles, as well as traditional Hollywood
releases.

The Wolfville Heritage Advisory
Committee has developed a self-guided walking tour of heritage properties, including the
old Dominion Atlantic Railway Station, which
was recently transformed into a beautiful new
public library and the Acadia Seminary. The
"Sem" was one of the first educational institu-
tions open to women in the British Empire
and is one of the oldest university buildings
still in use in Nova Scotia.

The north side of Wolfville is graced by the
soulful beauty of the dykelands built by early
Acadians and a postcard view of Cape
Blomidon, the famous promontory that is an
essential symbol of the land of Evangeline.
The wharf on the east end of Front Street is a
good observation point for the dramatic Fundy
tides and a favourite gathering place for sunset watchers. To the south, the Gaspereau
Valley offers a pastoral alternative route from
Wolfville east to Avonport.

The Acadians were the first Europeans to
settle in the area. They turned sea marsh into
fertile farmlands with an ingenious and complex technology. Eventually, dykes and
aboiteau, (the sluice designed to control the
flow of sea water) were built in all the marshland regions along the Minas Basin. After the
Expulsion in 1755, New England settlers were
brought in to farm the already well-cultivated
land, and they founded and developed the
settlement that became Wolfville.

The Mi'kmaq called it *Mtban* or Mud
Bridge, which meant "mud-catfish-catching
ground," because of a little brook that
flowed down from the South Mountain eventually mingling with the muddy tidal waters
from the Cornwallis River. When tides

drained the water away, there sat the mud.
Europeans called it Upper Horton then Mud
Creek. But the name became a source of
embarrassment for the uppercrust; eventually it was changed to honour the prominent
DeWolf family.

ATLANTIC THEATRE FESTIVAL

The question of whether a world-class theatre venue was to be or not to be in the town
of Wolfville was resolved in the summer of
1995 with the launching of the summer-long
Atlantic Theatre Festival and its three inaugural productions: Shakespeare's *The
Tempest*, George Feydeau's *A Flea in Her Ear*
and Anton Chekov's *The Cherry Orchard*.
Media attention was overwhelming considering the small town location. The *Globe and
Mail, Macleans*, and the CBC's Adrienne
Clarkson were amongst those who covered
the event. The participation of actor
Christopher Plummer gave further prestige to
an auspicious beginning.

The plays were indeed "the thing," but they
weren't everything. The theatre itself drew
rave reviews. The state-of-the-art 500 seat
playhouse on Main Street had its unlikely
beginnings as an abandoned ice rink. The
brilliant conversion has been compared to
Ontario's Stratford and New York's Circle in
the Round. Especially popular is the audience-
friendly thrust stage, one of only two in
Canada. For local people, it's a major cultural
event right in their own backyard.

The idea of a festival was conceived in a
Wolfville living room and then was brought to
fruition through the passionate determination
of artistic director and founder Michael
Bawtree and the strong support of the
community.

THE RESTAURANTS
Wolfville also has a growing reputation as one of *the* fine dining centres in the province. Discriminating diners come from the city to patronize establishments like Actons, Chez La Vigne, Blomidon Inn and the Tattingstone Inn—all of which were listed in the 1995 edition of *Where To Eat In Canada.*

The two inns mentioned are also noteworthy for their architecture, Blomidon being a fully restored nineteenth Century sea captain's mansion and Tattingstone a registered historic home of unrivalled elegance. Another charming inn—Victorian—was built for apple baron William H. Chase in 1893.

THE OLD BURYING GROUND
What is it that lures people to explore the sombre realm of old cemeteries—perhaps an intense curiosity inspired by our primordial fears, or is it simply that gravestones make for such fascinating reading?

Visit Wolfville's Old Burying Ground c.1774 on Main Street armed with a copy of *What Mean These Stones* by local author James Doyle Davison, especially if you're researching your roots. The book lists burial plots alphabetically by name, and by sections and rows, and provides information on people interred here. The author also provides some history of the site—a heritage property—and an in-depth account of a fairly recent and extensive restoration project. As well, Davison discusses burial customs and symbols (The broken branches carved on stone 116 symbolize a part of the tree of life, in memory of a three-year-old boy).

THE CHIMNEY SWIFTS
For the past few summers, Wolfville has been troubled by the mysterious disappearance of their beloved chimney swifts from the Robie

Tufts Nature Centre on Front Street. For unknown reasons the swift population dwindled drastically, giving their fans cause for alarm. As in Middleton, people had taken to gathering for the evening show—a whirlwind of chatty, acrobatic swifts circling the chimney at dusk, then suddenly, at some unknown signal, funnelling nimbly down into their roost. (Before civilization provided ready-made roosts, the tireless little swifts nested in hollow trees and branches.)

The Nature Centre, named after long-time Wolfville resident and renowned ornithologist Robie Tufts, who recorded swifts in the area as early as 1897, was created around an old dairy chimney, with the hope of attracting these appealing creatures. Swifts are easy to identify with their bow-and-arrow silhouette, their distinctive chattering call and their unique flying style—very fast wing beats that alternate with gliding. They are voracious insect-eaters who "dine on the fly," then return at the end of the day to rest on vertical surfaces with the help of spiny tail-quills.

Naturalists have tentatively blamed recently declining numbers of swifts on noise and the presence of merlin (pigeon hawks), which prey at dusk and early morning.

During spring migration and early summer of 1995, however, good swift-shows were reported at the Nature Centre, which bodes well for their return. When the swifts are flying, folks say, human spirits soar, too.

RANDALL HOUSE MUSEUM

Local residents have been enthusiastic donors to the Randall House Museum on Main Street, which exhibits an eclectic collection ranging from a stunning sterling silver flatware service for eighteen emblazoned with the DeWolf family crest, to hair wreaths, hats and sock dryers.

The house is open for public viewing, from the cool, dark, stone cellar to the oppressively hot attic (how *did* people ever sleep here in summer?), and visitors may touch the artifacts—but carefully.

Built around 1814 by coachmaker and church deacon Charles Randall, the late Georgian-style house looks much as it originally did.

The museum features numerous examples of nineteenth century needlework and cloth-ing, and a parlour designed to reflect the tradi-tion of preserving one room, unassaulted by children, that was suitable for weddings, funerals and an annual visit from the minister.

WOLFVILLE TO EVANGELINE BEACH
TANGLED GARDEN
Directions:

From Wolfville, drive east on Route 1 for almost 6 km (4 mi.). Tangled Garden is on the left.
Beverly McClare and George Walford have turned a scant acre of land in Grand Pré into a miniature paradise overflowing with herbs and flowers. McClare uses these plants and others that she gathers in local forests and fields to create organic baskets and sculptures. Herbs from the garden are blended into Tarragon Dill, Basil Wine and other tantalizing gourmet vinegars. Herbal jellies made careful-ly in small batches come in sophisticated flavours such as orange thyme, apple sage and quince rosemary.

Visitors are urged to stroll through the beautiful gardens, complete with goldfish and frog ponds. The gift shop has an appealing earthiness, with clusters of jewel-like, jelly-filled jars reflecting a flood of natural light. The walls are decorated with paintings by Walford, including textural abstracts that look right at home amidst the great bundles of colourful drying plants destined for McClare's creations.

EVANGELINE SNACK BAR
Directions:

From Wolfville, head east on Highway 1 to Grand Pré. The Evangeline Snack Bar is on the right, at the intersection of Highway 1 and Grand Pré Road.

Waistline be damned, it's hard to drive through Grand Pré on a beautiful late summer day without stopping at the Evangeline Snack Bar for a slice of Marjorie Stirling's heavenly home-made pie. We were too late in the season for peach, but cherry, apple and lemon were choice enough. Our cherry pie was served with a fork and a spoon so we wouldn't miss any of the tasty juice that puddles on the plate. Steaming coffee comes in big fine bone china mugs (we peeked at the bottom) and the menu also includes burgers, sandwiches, chowders and other old favourites.

Miss Stirling has baked her way into *Where to Eat in Canada,* and may be one of the few who had done so mainly on the merit of her home-made pies. The atmosphere is about as homey as it gets. The dishes and chairs don't match, and the walls are lined with a hodge-podge of china pieces, all for sale.

GRAND PRÉ NATIONAL HISTORIC SITE
Directions:

From Highway 101, take Exit 10 to Wolfville and drive west on Route 1 for 1 km (0.6 mi.), then north along Grand Pré Road for 1 km (0.6 mi.).

Acadian settlers from Port Royal came to the Minas Basin region in the 1680s armed with a passion for farming and with dyke-building skills honed in Port Royal. Reclaiming marshlands from scratch must have been a daunting task, unimaginable by

The stone church stands as a memorial to the Acadians and the 1755 Deportation.

today's mechanized standards. Back then farming required Herculean endurance and patience.

Rectangular sods were cut from the marshland and piled to form dykes that tapered from about four metres wide on the bottom to one metre on top, to a height of 1.5 m (5 ft) or so. Crops wouldn't grow until rain had helped leach sea salt from the soil. In the meantime, marsh grasses were gathered as salt hay fodder for livestock.

By the beginning of the eighteenth century, 105 families were living in settlements in the Minas Basin region, making it the most heavily populated area in the French colony of Acadia.

A visit to Grand Pré National Historic Site, which commemorates the Acadians and the Deportation, is an emotional experience. Even for those without Acadian roots, the terror of families being forced by British troops to leave their homes and land with only their personal belongings, is tangible. In less than a year, more than 6,000 Acadians were deported from Nova Scotia to points along the Eastern Seaboard, their burned villages and the magnificent dykelands the only things left behind. (A list of pre-Deportation Acadian names attracts many visitors.)

Evangeline Bellefontaine is the fictional heroine of an epic poem by H.W. Longfellow, the popular American poet of the nineteenth century. Ironically, he played an important role in inspiring sympathy for the Acadians, even though he never saw the region. The wistful Evangeline came to symbolize Acadian ideals of courage and faith, and her bronze statue watching over the commemorative church is a highlight of the park, as are the towering weeping willows believed to have sprung from cuttings brought by French settlers centuries ago.

Just beyond the park, a huge blue sign dryly imparts the statistics of beauty of the inspiring landscape poised before us: "Grand Pré Dyke, 3,013 acres below sea level behind 28,455 feet of dyke." It's easy to see why the Acadians named the area Grand Pré, meaning great meadow. The road slices through the legendary dykelands, prized for their fertility and their beauty. Maintained by the Nova Scotia Department of Agriculture and Marketing, the region is home to muskrats, moles and mink, and the birds that prey on them, including short-eared owls, northern harriers, American kestrels, red-tailed hawks and bald eagles.

EVANGELINE BEACH
Directions:
From Grand Pré National Historic Park, drive across the dykes to the next intersection. Turn left

*and follow the signs to Evangeline Beach, about
another 2 km (1.2 mi.).*

Don't be deceived by the lifeless appearance of
the mudflats. The vast, still expanse is actually
the cradle for a teeming population of marine
life, including clams, worms and mud shrimp.

From late summer through early fall, hundreds of thousands of migratory shorebirds
leave their arctic breeding grounds and congregate along the Minas Basin. Evangeline
Beach, Starr's Point and the Windsor
Causeway mudflats are special hot spots. Most
noticeable, for its overwhelming numbers, is
the tiny semipalmated sandpiper. The best
time to observe the birds is at high tide when
they congregate to form what biologists call "a
grey carpet of semis." Frantic feeding on crustaceans and worms can double their body
weight in a week or two; fat and rested, they
are then ready for the non-stop flight to win-
tering grounds in South America.

Other shorebirds to look for are black-
bellied and semipalmated plovers, the large,
impressive Hudsoniangodwit, dowitchers,
greater and lesser yellowlegs, ruddy turn-
stones, sanderlings, dunlins and least and
white-rumped sandpipers.

Against the a striking backdrop of
Blomidon, birds stalk the intertidal zone (the
area between high tide and low tide) feeding
on invertebrates burrowed in the sticky stuff.
Lucky shorebird-watchers may also spy two
kinds of falcons—merlin and peregrine.

Before the turn of the century when natural
resources seemed inexhaustible, Evangeline
Beach was also a major shad-fishing area. Stubs
of birch poles used for gill-nets can still be seen
nearby.

Mudlarking isn't for everyone but it can be
great fun for the young at heart. (The really
brave go mud-slidding during the incoming
tide.) Beachcombing on the mudflats requires

a sense of humour and a decided lack of decorum. Some prefer bare feet, while others are leery of barnacles and similar hidden hazards. Urged by the antics of an uninhibited five-year-old, we were reduced to near-hysterical laughter by our clownish, mud-caked feet, which grew bigger with every step. By the time our struggle to the water's edge ended, we were hopelessly mucky. No amount of cautious tiptoeing could evade the magnetic nature of the mud. Plodding back, we zigzagged to every puddle on the beach, trying to leave most of the ooze behind.

WOLFVILLE TO CAPE BLOMIDON AND CAPE SPLIT LOOP

Directions:

From Wolfville, head west on Highway 1 to Greenwich, keeping an eye peeled for farm markets brimming with fresh produce, then turn right to Port Williams on Route 358. Set aside a day for this excursion through the backroads of a region known for its beautiful scenery and valued heritage.

The route twists and turns, sometimes sharply, and some of the roads have no signposts, but don't worry about missing a turn or two. With the Minas shoreline and Blomidon as landmarks, you're not likely to lose your bearings. And if you do get a bit lost, we found it just proved the adage that you discover things you otherwise wouldn't have.

The parking area next to the bridge in Port Williams is a good place to mark the dramatic rise and fall of the tides. Make a mental note of the water line, and when you return from your day trip, you'll see why the Bay of Fundy tides, the highest on earth, are so renowned.

In the village, watch for the road on the

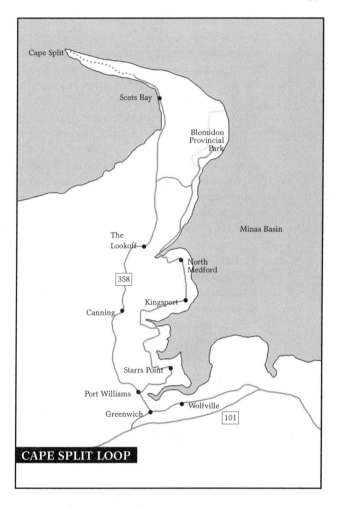

CAPE SPLIT LOOP

right heading to Starrs Point. Here begins a beautiful journey—through dykelands and farmlands, past elegant homes and heritage properties, beaches and wonderful shoreline views—that left us mildly envious of those who live here. When the road bears sharply left, you get your first peek at the Minas Basin; throughout the drive it blinks in and out of sight as the road coils towards Blomidon. We weren't satisfied until we reached the provincial park and dipped our toes in the ocean, no matter that it was well into October.

Another attraction is the abundance of U-picks. Load up with apples pulled fresh from the tree and you'll be ready for impromptu picnics throughout the day. Willowbank Farm has U-pick raspberries in July and apples starting Labour Day Weekend. The U-pick pumpkin patch is open until Halloween, and there's also a collection of antique horse-drawn carriages on display. We had a picnic of apples, cheese and French bread, then explored the farm, feeding fistfuls of clover to the horses and llamas that forage about the fields.

PRESCOTT HOUSE

Apple lovers have Charles Prescott to thank for many of the varieties—especially the tart, snappy Gravenstein—that Nova Scotia is famous for. A politician and businessman until forced to retire by poor health, Prescott turned his interests to horticulture, and eventually introduced more than one hundred new varieties of apples using a process of testing and trial. Known for his sociable and generous nature, he shared shoots and buds without reservation. Today, Kings County accounts for ninety percent of all apple production in the province.

Prescott settled at Starr's Point in the early 1800s, in a custom-built, classic Georgian-style brick mansion warmed by seven fireplaces. Hothouses and gardens reflected his passion for growing. At least twenty-seven varieties of apples could be found in his orchards, including Gravenstein, Northern Spy and Ribston Pippin.

After his death in 1859, the estate fell into neglect, at one point housing itinerant labourers. In 1930, one of Prescott's great-granddaughters purchased and restored the property, which became part of the Nova

Scotia Museum system in 1971. Open from
June to mid-October, admission is free.

Each fall the museum hosts an apple display with as many varieties as can be found in
local orchards, and visitors are surveyed for
their preferences. Picking a favourite isn't
easy. Hundreds of varieties have been grown
in Nova Scotia over the years; while Winter
Banana, Seek-no-further, Pumpkin Sweet,

Rose Red and other equally exotic-sounding
varieties may not have caught our fancy, Nova
Scotians still have an undiminished passion
for honoured apples.

After visiting the museum, we drove on
past farms and apple trees in various stages of
development. In recent years, valley orchards
have been in flux, with farmers increasing
Northern Spy production to meet the demands
of a thriving local pie producer. Dating back to
1840, the Northern Spy has become prized by

Prescott House, c1814, is furnished with period antiques and surrounded by extensive gardens.

the baking industry because it keeps its shape during cooking.

After a right turn on Wellington Dyke Road, we parked beside a large blue sign announcing: "Wellington Dyke. Protecting 3030 acres from high tide. First protected in 1812." The spectacular scenery, commonplace in this region, is a rare sight to an eye from away. Wellington Dyke was built by the New England Planters to extend the Acadians' dyke system.

As early as 1672, great quantities of wheat were being harvested from dyked lands along the Annapolis Basin. But if not for the dykes, the natural intertidal mudflats would blanket thousands of hectares of potentially productive farmland and residential areas in the vicinity of Grand Pré, Wolfville, Port Williams and Canard. Over history, eighty-five percent of the Bay of Fundy's salt marshes have been converted to agricultural land.

As with any natural area, it's wise to respect the environmental fragility of the salt marshes, mudflats and dykelands. The unique flora and fauna can be observed by carefully venturing on to the dyke with an ear tuned to the sounds of sharp-tailed sparrows, marsh harriers, horned larks, semipalmated sandpipers, black-bellied plovers and many other birds, according to the season. Salt-tolerant plants such as sea lavender, cordgrasses and glasswort have adapted to survive occasional drenching in sea water.

Proceed to the next intersection, then turn right on to Canard Street, left on Saxon Street and right at the Canning Aboiteau road. At the stop sign, turn right onto Route 221 to Kingsport, once a major shipbuilding port. (A left turn leads to the village of Canning, where food, lodging, stores and service stations can be found). At Kingsport, watch for the sharp bend in the road at Water Street and the old

Kingsport wharf. Here you will find a public picnic area and easy access to the beach.

Continue along Water Street to the stop sign and turn left onto Longspell Road. At the next stop sign, turn right to Medford. The scenery is still a unique mixture of ocean vistas and agricultural productivity, where apple orchards, potato fields, and spectacular seascapes harmonize. To get close to the shoreline, turn right at Medford Beach Road and park at the shore. To the right, a rough path leads down to the beach. Although extremely rare, dinosaur fossils and tracks have been found in this area.

Return to the Medford Road and continue to the next stop sign, then turn left on the North Medford Road. At the next stop sign, turn right towards the forested mountain and continue for a short distance on a good gravel road. The road drops rather steeply and actually dips below sea level at the bottom, where the dykes momentarily obscure the view of the shore. Turn right at the next stop sign onto the paved Pereau Road.

Scenes of small inlets and grassy marshlands are ideal photo opportunities. The Pereau (Delhaven) wharf, with its brightly painted fishing boats, and Paddy's Island in the distance, will have shutter-bugs grabbing for cameras. Apple orchards next to fishing wharves embody the essence of the region. Farmlands leading to Blomidon seem postcard-perfect, even those with old barns crumbling to the ground and house shingles rubbed raw by the wind.

In spring when the earth is freshly plowed into corduroy patterns, and the ocean forms a backdrop for the rich, reddish-brown fields, people often marvel at the perfect union of land and sea. The road ends at Blomidon Provincial Park, where camping, hiking, picnicking and beachcombing draw visitors to the area, the legendary home of the Mi'kmaq god Glooscap.

BLOMIDON PROVINCIAL PARK

There's a lot to be learned from the demeanour of the porcupines that forage lackadaisically throughout the park. They've become used to sharing their space with humans, and in turn, most people react to the scavengers with patient amusement. There is, after all, plenty of room for everyone. The park, sprawled on the rugged promontory of Cape Blomidon overlooking the Minas Basin, encompasses 750 ha (1,875 acres). Varied habitats—forests, mudflats, swamp, fen and bog—support an equally diverse community of wildlife, including white-tail deer, bobcat, bear, coyote, bald eagles and showshoe hare.

A 13.7 km (8.5 mi.) system of interconnected trails provides access to a variety of habitats and scenic look-offs.

Blomidon tides have a range of 12 m (40 ft) and rise fast—1 m (3 ft) in only twenty minutes. For that reason, shore walkers are warned to check local tide tables. Leave the car in the parking area at the entrance to the park, then follow the path through the picnic area, down some wooden stairs and onto the beach.

It's said that the fourteen billion tons of sea water that flow into the Minas Basin twice daily causes the countryside to actually tilt slightly under the load, an undetectable phenomenon that didn't worry us a bit as we padded through the gentle surf.

This is an ideal place to gain an appreciation of nature's power to rapidly erode the sandstone shoreline. Tree roots left grasping at air on cliff-tops speak volumes.

People love roaming this beach and wading in the tepid surf. Water is heated as it flows over the sun-warmed sand, but it cools off quickly the farther out you go. We doffed our shoes to feel the pudding-like mud between our toes. Children can spend hours poking around for clams, periwinkles, mussels and barnacles, and drawing lines in the sand to mark the speed of the incoming tide. Harbour porpoises, Atlantic white-sided dolphins and harbour seals are some of the marine mammals that pursue their meals into the Minas Basin. The basin mudflats are also important feeding areas for migratory shorebirds during summer low tides and for ground fish such as flounders and skates.

Even when the park is closed for the season, the lower picnic area, the beach and the park trails remain accessible, and Blomidon's spectacular beauty draws people here at any time of year.

Leaving the park, backtrack on the same road, but keep an eye out for Stewart Mountain Road on the right, just after the big green house with the flat roof. On this steep, winding gravel road you'll be quickly taken away from the lush farming area and up into the rugged terrain of the North Mountain. At the next stop sign, turn right on Route 358 towards Scots Bay.

SCOTS BAY

I've been to this isolated community when clear, blue skies and calm seas seem to promise eternal tranquillity, only to return and find the village embroiled in a tempest, with furious waves clobbering the basalt shore and fishing wharf.

Scots Bay, (named for a group of Scottish immigrants who were driven ashore by a storm), Cape Split and Cape Blomidon form one of the most recognizable landforms along the Nova Scotia coastline—a sharp, aggressive-looking hook that slices hard into the Minas Basin and a distinctive promontory that towers above the shore.

Rockhounders flock to the Scots Bay area famous for deposits of agates (the provincial gemstone), amethysts, chalcedony and zeolites such as mesolite, natrolite and stilbite. But resist the urge to stuff your pockets, because there's "limited collecting only," meaning just one or two specimens of each stone.

According to *A Natural History of Kings County,* published by the Blomidon Naturalists Society, the treasure trove was left here by Jurassic-age volcanic basalts, and cold weather makes more stones available each spring: "In winter, ice forms in the cracks of fractured rocks and further breaks and loosens them. Each spring the new rock falls contain many treasures for rock hounds."

DEE DEE'S DINETTE & MALT SHOPPE

Justin Tait says he was simply fulfilling destiny when he and his partner Patricia Whitty opened Dee Dee's Dinette on Route 358 in Scots Bay and began filling it with a personal collection of hundreds of antique toys.

The seasonal diner is just the kind of unusual, out-of-the-way place that is a real delight to stumble upon. The food is classic diner fare, but the couple makes it something special. Even the hot dogs are extraordinary, capped with unique garnishes and toppings. The muffins, tea biscuits and brownies, all homemade, are enormous, the Belgium waffles come with fruit and cream, and the French toast is "Pat's World Famous."

Most people are startled to discover this funky, folky, hand-painted establishment along this rugged coast, but the element of surprise is a major attraction. Traffic to the famed hiking trail at nearby Cape Split can get pretty heavy, and Dee Dee's is a weird and wonderful pit stop, decorated with flea market finds, a huge collection of menus and postcards, and a free pinball machine.

Justin describes the dinette's atmosphere as "tongue-in-cheek with an element of seriousness," an assessment clearly reflected in the small library where everything from existentialism to Popeye the Sailor can be found. But go for the food.

CAPE SPLIT

Once in Scots Bay, follow the road along the shore to Cape Split, one of the province's most popular and spectacular hiking trails. About half a day is required to walk the 13 km (8 mi.) distance.

Private ownership of the land, and physical features that call for a great deal of caution in some spots, do little to discourage visitors.

The trail offers a mixture of wooded and grassy terrain and opportunities to enjoy rare plants, as well as a myriad of mushrooms and fungi. In late May, the forest floor is blanketed with spring flowers like Dutchman's breeches, red trillium, pink lady's-slippers and violets—but please don't pick them.

At the head of the cape, the cliffs tower some 90 m (300 ft) above the rocky shoreline. Far below, plucky black guillemot use their wings as well as their bright red legs and feet to race underwater after small fish and shrimp. Herring gulls, great black-backed gulls and double-crested cormorants nest at the tip of the cape. This is also a good place to watch incoming flood tides, which gather momentum in Scots Bay, then rush furiously around Cape Split.

From Cape Split, Route 358 south takes us straight to the Lookoff, where you'll be treated to an eagle's-eye view of much of the area covered in your day trip.

THE LOOKOFF

With scenery this dazzling, who cares that we're standing on 200-million-year-old basaltic lava flows, and that the lava poured out when North America began to break away from Africa as the supercontinent Pangea rifted apart. Geologists tell us Devonian granites 370 million years old underlie the South Mountain on the skyline, and that the Triassic-age sandstones and shales were eroded with ease by glaciers and running water to create the valley floor. From an elevation of 205 m (675 ft), we're simply stunned by the beauty of it all. Far below, miniaturized farm machinery works the earth into patchwork squares of alternating colours and textures.

Even long-time residents never tire of piling in the car and roaring up the North Mountain to the Lookoff, where the seasons, the weather and the constantly moving Fundy tides create an ever-changing spectacle.

Continue south on Route 358, which soon begins to wind its way down the North Mountain, towards the village of Canning.

HOLLY CARR AND ALAN BATEMAN STUDIO

Along the way, you might want to drop in on artists Holly Carr and Alan Bateman, who welcome visitors to their 200-year-old farmhouse studio nestled on ten lush acres—an environment that inspires creativity, the couple happily acknowledges. Turn right on to Woodside Road and drive 3.2 km (2 mi.) to house #299 on the right-hand side of the road.

Holly Carr creates art that you can wrap around your neck or hang on your wall. She paints silk clothing, scarves, wall-hangings, pillows and pictures ranging from social satire to bold florals. Plump cherubs, dragonflies, giraffes and bespectacled old ladies have all made their way into paintings on crepe and pongee silk. It's a rare day when a piece of pure, unbleached white silk won't be found on the stretcher, with Holly hand-painting in freehand some new design. Her husband, Alan Bateman, paints rural landscapes and objects in a realistic style using watercolours and acrylics.

After the studio, return to Route 358 and continue to the village of Canning.

Monuments serve a dual purpose in towns and villages: they provide some local history in a public setting and they're good reference points for directions—"turn left at the monument." Canning's Borden Monument honours the memory of Lieut. Harold Lothrup Borden, a third-year medical student at McGill University when he was killed in the Boer War while serving with the Canadian Mounted Rifles. He was the only son of Canning's Sir Frederick Borden, then Minister of Militia. Unveiled in 1903, the monument depicts scenes from the Boer War, and was functionally designed with a trough on one side for passing horses.

Once a famous shipbuilding port and agricultural export centre known as Apple Tree Landing, Canning has been rediscovered as a tourist destination with hospitable lodging, interesting shops and good places to eat—among them Bellhill Tea House, The Front Porch Cafe, the Farmhouse Inn and Apple Tree Studio (an art gallery and gift shop). E. L. Newcomb's china shop is full of fragile delights—bone china plates, tea cups and knickknacks—while the old-fashioned Village Meat Store with its massive butcher block rippled by years of use, peddles substantial home-made sausages and thick slabs of prime beef.

From December to March, Canning and the neighbouring community of Sheffield Mills are excellent territory for observing bald eagles. Trees around farmyards become observation posts for eagles looking for carrion. In turn, humans clutching binoculars gather nearby to watch the big birds tearing at chunks of poultry and other carcasses with their powerful beaks and talons. Each year, the Sheffield Mills community hall celebrates with a pancake breakfast and guided tours of eagle hot spots. In 1994, 440 bald eagles were counted in eastern Kings County in a single day.

From Canning, Route 358 will take you back to Highway 1. Turn left for Wolfville and Grand Pré, or right for New Minas and Kentville.

HANTS

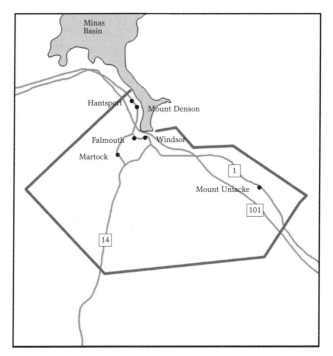

HANTSPORT

Take Exit 8 off Highway 101, then turn left on Route 1 heading west.

The affluence of Hantsport's grand shipbuilding era is still palpable in this small, charming town. Located on the Avon River about 2 km (1.2 mi.) from the Minas Basin, Hantsport was, in 1895, the smallest incorporated town in Canada, yet one of the largest shipbuilding centres in the world. In its heyday, over two hundred large wooden barques, brigs and schooners were built and repaired here at its two major shipyards.

110

Memories of those days are evoked by historic homes and landmarks like the Churchill House. Shipyard magnate and Senator Ezra Churchill enlisted skilled ships carpenters to create this classic Victorian-style mansion as a wedding gift for his son, John, in 1860.

Hantsport, located on the Avon River, has a rich ship-building heritage.

Money was no object judging by the marble fireplaces, French crystal chandeliers, opulent Belgium diamond dust mirrors, oak and mahogany floors and elegantly embossed leather wallcoverings. Years later, George Lyons, an imaginative craftsman from nearby Falmouth, was called in to further embellish the interior. His elaborately hand-painted floral designs and beautifully sculpted mouldings, (restored in 1966), are a joy to behold.

Quaint Santa Claus and Mother Goose figures still frolic on the walls of the former nursery, now used to display marine and shipbuilding artifacts.

Francis Silver, a Portuguese native who became one of Churchill's favourite craftsmen, amused himself, and countless others, by painting scenes of everyday life on the basement walls of the Churchill home and in the Carriage House located on the estate. Silver has since been recognized as a significant Nova Scotia folk artist, and while the paintings from the Carriage House are now on display at the Art Gallery of Nova Scotia, you can still see his fanciful work in the basement— from landscapes to exotic birds and castles.

From the big, square widow's walk the Avon River is barely visible for the trees, but in Churchill's time this was a favourite retreat, a place to savour a good cigar and survey the river and the town.

Today, the house doubles as a community centre, an arrangement that has created, in some parts of the building, an odd-looking union of old and new.

Fundy Gypsum Company is a huge presence in the town, occupying a large chunk of the waterfront. Gypsum and anhydrite (calcium sulphate) mined in nearby Windsor and shipped to the plant by rail, are blasted and crushed together to pieces less than 15 cm (6 in.) in size, then separated using a process by which the anhydrite sinks and the gypsum floats. Once processed, the minerals are packed aboard massive vessels for export.

Save for a lone Great Blue Heron stalking the shoreline, we found the waterfront strangely quiet the Saturday we were in town. Had we been lucky we might have seen a tugboat guiding one of the huge freighters into dock. Up to twenty-four tons of gypsum is loaded in less than three hours, so the ship can sail on the turn of the tide.

JANET POPE
Directions:
Take exit 8 off Highway 101, then turn right at the end of the access road toward Mount Denson. Janet lives in the gold house on the left at the top of the first hill.

Visit the studio of renowned fabric artist Janet Pope with scrubbed hands and you may be invited to run your fingers gently over her richly textured, vibrantly coloured wallhangings and quilts. Many are created from men's neckties that she buys in bulk, washes, then rips apart to use in sensational hangings that shout love for all aspects of nature, from earth, wind and fire to animals and insects. By touching, you'll gain an even keener sense of the intensity with which this effervescent artist works, and the skill of hands that can manipulate fabric into such exuberant images.

Bales of hay are ready for gathering on a farm in Falmouth.

Paintings by Janet's late brother, Robert Pope, are on display throughout her home, (headquarters, as well, of the publishing company Lancelot Press, founded by her family), which has a commanding view of the tide-driven Avon River and the sprawling gypsum wharf across the way.

FALMOUTH: SAINTE FAMILLE WINES
Directions:

From Highway 101, take Exit 7, then just follow the blue signs with the cluster of grapes. They'll lead you right to the winery.

The sourish, earthy aroma of fermenting grapes greets you as you step into the Sainte Famille gift shop. The adjacent production area contains gleaming vats, tubes and other equipment used to make white and red wines from grapes such as Marachel Foch, Michurnetz, Chardonnay and Riesling, grown on the surrounding 9 ha (23 acre) family farm.

The operation is named for *La Paroisse Sainte Famille De Pisiguit,* an original Acadian village site settled around 1685 upon which the vineyard and winery are located.

Farm wineries are becoming popular tourist destinations. We enjoyed standing at the "bar" sipping wines and cleansing our palates in between with plain crackers, served by the congenial, well-informed staff. A wine list offers serving suggestions and rates the wines according to their dryness, from dry dinner wines to semi-sweet dessert wines. We liked the Dry Riesling—"done in the Alsatian style," we were informed—with a nose of clover and flowers, and a clean, citrusy taste.

There are free tours of the production area and vineyards, and the retail shop carries a full selection of wines and gift items.

WINDSOR

Directions:

Exit 6 from Highway 101 leads straight to down-town Windsor.

Sculptors make frequent pilgrimages to the Windsor area for chunks of soft, carvable gypsum, in colours from very white to grey, brown, blue and a beautiful black. While the mineral isn't exclusive to the region, it's more conspicuous and accessible here than else-where in the province.

Crossing the causeway at the mouth of the Avon River estuary near Windsor at low tide is like traversing an alien landscape. The gleaming mudflats seem lunar-like, spiked with tufts of marshgrass and riddled with curious mud-figures moulded by the ebbing water.

Windsor is "well known" for so many

114

things that you can take your pick. In recent years, the famed giant pumpkins of Howard Dill have come to rival the celebrity of Windsor's two most famous sons—Sam Slick, (the town's trademark character), and his renowned creator, Thomas Chandler Haliburton. At least one tourist publication says the tidal bore is Windsor's "most famous attraction." Some people say the slick, sprawling mudflats at the causeway best define

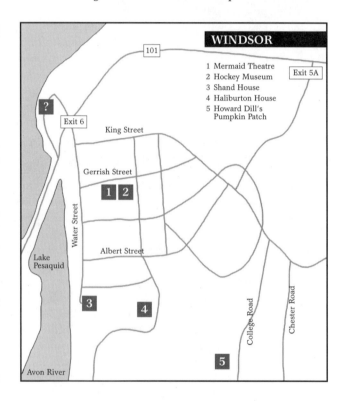

Windsor. Add to these the Mermaid Theatre, Shand House (an elaborate 1891 mansion, now part of the NS Museum complex), the Hants County Exhibition (Canada's oldest agricultural fair), the Windsor Pumpkin Festival, Haliburton House, the Fort Edward Blockhouse, the Windsor Country Fair, King's

Edgehill (the oldest private educational insti-
tute in the British Commonwealth) and the
new Windsor Hockey Heritage Museum—just
to name a few—and disagreement is assured.

This community of multiple singularities is
further distinguished by its unusually high
percentage of brick buildings—a distinction
born of disaster. Windsor has twice risen from
the ashes of two horrific fires; the fire of 1897
ended the town's sway as one of the
Maritimes principal business centres.

WINDSOR HOCKEY
HERITAGE MUSEUM

Long before the days of franchised sports
stores and the NHL, kids used to wallop
frozen potatoes, boot heels, lumps of coal and
discs cut from tree branches around frozen
ponds with wooden sticks. It all began in
Windsor, say members of the Windsor Hockey
Heritage Society, who have gathered plenty of
evidence to support the town's claim to be the
birthplace of hockey. Garth Vaughan, a local
doctor and hockey enthusiast, began the cam-
paign to prove that Canada's national game
originated on the ice of Long Pond (located,
coincidentally, on Howard Dill's farm), and
that students of King's College School were
the first to play the game in Canada, sometime around 1800. By the beginning of the
twentieth century, Windsor—with a population of only two thousand—had four major
teams competing for the Citizens Trophy.

Those curious to know how hockey got its
name, where the first covered rinks were built
and who handcrafted the first hockey sticks
from tree branches will want to visit
Windsor's new Hockey Heritage Museum on
Gerrish Street, a goldmine of hockey lore.
Displays illustrate the evolution of the game,
from the days when skates were little more
than wooden platforms fixed with crude hand-

fashioned metal runners and provided trans-
portation along frozen streams and riverways.

The Hockey Heritage Society's other goals
include building an arena for year-round use
and establishing a hockey school.

THE MERMAID THEATRE

Next door to the museum, a lighthearted
storefront marks the home of Nova Scotia's
world-famous puppet performers, the
Mermaid Theatre. One of the province's major
cultural employers, the theatre presents
unique adaptations of *Puss in Boots, Gulliver's
Travels, Stuart Little* and other children's clas-
sics to audiences around the globe.

SAM SLICK

Sam Slick was a Yankee clockmaker from
Slickville, U.S.A., who had a penchant for
catchy sayings. "The early bird gets the
worm," "Fact is stranger than fiction," "Seeing
is believing" and "Raining cats and dogs" are
just a few of the phrases coined by the
fictitious character who sprang from the
imagination of Windsor native, Judge Thomas
Chandler Haliburton.

Haliburton was perhaps the first Canadian
author to gain international reputation, and
the rascally Sam was his most famous creation. In his day (1796-1865), his popularity is
said to have rivalled that of Charles Dickens.
Almost forgotten is that he was a judge, and
that he drew on the local population for much
of his material, especially those who landed in
the courtroom of "the joking judge," as he
came to be known.

The elegant one-and-a-half storey villa on
Clifton Avenue, where Haliburton did much
of his writing, is now a branch of the Nova
Scotia Museum and a popular tourist attraction, although it has undergone considerable
change since his time. The judge and his wife,

Louisa, shared a passion for gardening that is reflected still in the spacious grounds.

HOWARD DILL AND
HIS GIANT PUMPKINS
Directions:
From Exit 6 off Highway 101 entering Windsor, turn left on King Street, then right on College Road.

After a visit to the farm of Howard Dill, the world-famous "pumpkin king," we left wondering which had been more fun, the pumpkins or the man who grows them. Growing giant pumpkins started as a hobby, and since he's just doing what he likes, Dill still wonders what all the fuss is about.

Despite the attention lavished upon him (He has appeared on the cover of four American magazines, been featured on prime-time U.S. television and is listed in the book *Canadian Achievers* along with the likes of Anne Murray, Terry Fox and Rita McNeil), he remains charming and unpretentious and not at all stingy with stories, or even his growing tips: "I gave my secrets away years ago," he told us with a grin.

World Champion four times in a row, Dill's first behemoth (in 1979) weighed 199 kg (438.5 lbs) and was greeted with amazement. But the Windsor farmer had started a craze, and today's specimens are stratospheric. In 1994 an Ontario man set a world record with a massive 990 pounder!

Howard Dill now devotes much of his energy to reproducing pumpkin seeds, including his trademark and patented Dill's Atlantic Giant, which can be bought at the farm. In the fall, tour buses and school kids arrive for special displays.

True to expectations, early fall visitors are greeted by a cheery sight: a vine-scattered pumpkin patch packed with chunky orange globes of all shapes and sizes. Dill claims that "pumpkins have the power to make people happy," and he actively implements his philosophy; he shipped Canadians serving in the Gulf War a walloping 205 kg (450 lb) morale-booster. But does it follow that the bigger the pumpkin, the stronger its magic? Seeing a grinning two-year old clutching a miniature pumpkin no bigger than an apple convinced us that size has nothing to do with it.

Sample delicious pies at the Windsor Pumpkin Festival.

THE WINDSOR PUMPKIN FESTIVAL

Don't expect the pumpkins on display at the Windsor Pumpkin Festival to look like larger versions of the cheerful, symmetrical little orange ones we've come to know and love. In straining towards record-breaking size, they have turned into colossal, ungainly monstrosities. They may have lost their perky cuteness, but not their appeal, as proven by the throngs that gather each October to marvel at them.

The festival doubles as Weigh-off Day for the World Pumpkin Confederation, an event held simultaneously at other locations around the globe.

Music, handcrafts and, of course, pumpkin pie are all part of the fun.

WINDSOR TO MOUNT UNIACKE

At Windsor, Highway 101 barrels inland towards sparser, scragglier terrain, leaving the fertile valley floor behind. Seams of gypsum crop up everywhere. White cliffs (the visible part of gypsum deposits) iced with evergreen trees are visible on the left where the highway crosses the St. Croix River. Gypsum Ragwort and the rare Yellow Lady's Slipper—both calcium-loving plants—flower here early in summer.

In the early 1900s gypsum, deposits were left when inland seas evaporated some 350 million years ago, was the chief item of trade in the Windsor area.

Traffic climbs the long slope to the upland. Near Mount Uniacke the road toys with the eastern edge of granite country, a region that extends unbroken to southern Yarmouth County. Thin, rocky soil barely covers the slates and granites. To escape the monotony of the highway, we headed towards the lush environment of the Uniacke Estate Museum Park.

UNIACKE ESTATE MUSEUM PARK
Directions:
Take Exit 3 off Highway 101. Turn left at Highway 1 (at the Irving Station), proceed about 8 km (5 mi.). Watch for the main entranceway on the left.
Built in 1813 on the old post road from Windsor to Halifax, Uniacke House is shaded from the highway by thick woods and a long, gravel driveway sheltered by a mantle of trees. The estate's original 4,400 ha (11,000 acres) have dwindled over the years to 1,000 (2,500).

Richard John Uniacke, a prominent Halifax lawyer who went on to become Attorney General of Nova Scotia, built the lovely rambling estate as a summer retreat. Born in

County Cork, Ireland, he arrived in Nova
Scotia around 1775, married his new employ-
er's twelve-year-old daughter (They had a
dozen children), and proceeded to lead a
colourful and financially lucrative life.

Uniacke first set eyes on the site of his
future summer home at the age of 23 while
being brought to Halifax as a prisoner charged
with treason following the Cumberland
Rebellion (The charges were later dropped).
Tradition says he stopped to rest at the lake
with his guards and declared the surroundings
reminiscent of his family home in Ireland. A
decade later, as a rising political figure, he
began acquiring land along the shore of the
lake, which he later named for Martha, his
wife. Construction on the country house started when he turned sixty.

After Uniacke's death in 1830, the property
stayed in the family until 1949 when it was
acquired by the province.

Little of the house and its contents have
changed since Uniacke's time, which makes
this estate a rare treat. Subsequent generations
resisted modernization, and the original decor
remains virtually intact, including Mahogany
furniture imported from London and an
eighteenth-century creamware dessert service
that once belonged to Prince Edward, father
of the future Queen Victoria.

A massive four-poster bed and oversize
custom-made armchair are reminders that
Uniacke was a big man, tall and wide.

In an effort to maintain historic integrity
the house receives most of its light naturally, a
feature that can be frustrating on dark, rainy
days such as the one on which we visited.

Recently, the Nova Scotia Museum developed six walking trails of various lengths and
terrains, which lead to points of interest
around the estate.

The trails range from the thirty-minute-long Lake Martha Loop—a hardpacked gravel path running along woodland and lakeshore, suitable for families and casual strollers—to the challenging Wetlands Trail, which takes about six hours and winds through natural habitats, including two lakes, a beaver dam and huge boulders left behind by glaciers.

The Uniacke home is open from June 1 to October 15; the trails can be used year round although they are not kept clear in winter.

BIBLIOGRAPHY

Allen, C.R.K. *Yarmouth County: A Naturalist Notebook.* Halifax: Nimbus, 1987.

Bird, Will R. *Off-Trail in Nova Scotia.* Toronto: Ryerson Press, 1956.

Blomidon Naturalists Society. *A Natural History of Kings County, Nova Scotia.* Wolfville: Acadia University, 1992.

Bull, Mary Kate. *Sandy Cove.* Hantsport: Lancelot, 1978.

Davison, James Doyle. *Mud Creek: The Story of the Town of Wolfville, Nova Scotia.* Wolfville Historical Society, 1985.

Davison, James Doyle. *What Mean These Stones.* Wolfville: Heritage Advisory Committee, 1990.

Heritage Trust of Nova Scotia. *Seasoned Timbers, Vol. 1. A Sampling of Historic Buildings Unique to Western Nova Scotia.* 1972.

Hutten, Anne. *Valley Gold.* Halifax: Petheric Press, 1981.

Kingsbury, Al. *The Pumpkin King—Four Time World Champion Howard Dill and the Atlantic Giant.* Hantsport: Lancelot Press, 1992.

Mitcham, Allison. *Paradise or Purgatory: Island Life in Nova Scotia and New Brunswick.* Hantsport: Lancelot, 1992.

Nichols, Mabel. *The Devil's Half Acre.* Kentville Centennial Committee, 1986.

Norwood, Caroline B. *Life on Brier Island Nova Scotia.* Westport: Norwood Publishing, 1995.

Public Archives of Nova Scotia. *Place Names and Places in Nova Scotia.* 1967.

Ross, Sally and Alphonse Deveau. *The Acadians of Nova Scotia Past and Present.* Halifax: Nimbus, 1992.

Sauer, Julia L. *Fog Magic.* New York: Viking Penguin, 1943.

Shea, Phil. *Brier Island: Land's End in the Bay of Fundy.* Hantsport: Lancelot, 1990.

Stephens, David E. *Lighthouses of Nova Scotia.* Windsor: Lancelot Press, 1973.

Thurston, Harry. *Tidal Life: A Natural History of the Bay of Fundy.* Ontario: Camden House Publishing, 1990.

———. *Against the Storm: Lighthouses of the Northeast.* Halifax: Nimbus, 1993.

Woodman, Harold. *A Pictorial History of the Apple Blossom Festival.* Hantsport: Lancelot Press, 1992.